The Collected Poems of Ursula Vaughan Williams

Ursula Vaughan Williams

[illegible], with greetings from

Ursula

30 January 1998.

Albion Music Limited

First edition 1996

ISBN 0 9528706 0 6

Published by
Albion Music Limited

A Division of the Ralph Vaughan Williams Society

Printed in England

The Collected Poems
of
Ursula Vaughan Williams

URSULA VAUGHAN WILLIAMS

Introduction

Ursula Vaughan Williams was born in Malta in 1911. With a strong military background, her early years were inevitably spent on the move – Plymouth, Woolwich, Leeds and Blackheath, for example. Leaving school at 17, she attended finishing school in Brussels where she was able to visit the opera, theatre and art galleries establishing the interest in music, literature and art which has remained to this day.

In 1932, she had the opportunity to become a student at the Old Vic Theatre Company. In the same week that she auditioned at the Old Vic, she became engaged to Captain (later Lieutenant-Colonel) Michael Wood. They married in 1933.

Ursula had began writing poetry at the age of ten. The earliest poem in this Collection is *The Mountaineer*, written in 1927. Her first published collection appeared in 1941 under the title *No Other Choice*. Further collections were published in 1943 and 1948. Ursula has also written four novels, three of which have been published.

Following the death of her husband, Michael, in 1942, Ursula's friendship with the composer, Ralph Vaughan Williams, deepened. They married in 1953.

Whilst Ursula Vaughan Williams does not belong to any school of poetry, the influence of certain writers can be detected in her work. She had discovered Yeats in 1925–26, and his impact can be noted in the stylish and subtle imagery which distinguishes her work. It is, perhaps, Thomas Hardy who is most frequently remembered when reading Ursula's poetry, especially in the range of formal structures adopted, in the flexible metres and in the evocative and atmospheric tone.

Her poetry appeals to musicians: it has been set by over 30 composers. As Roger Steptoe put it:

> "There is a beauty to it. It is very sensitive. She can capture moods and ideas in a few words or lines. Above all, the words are evocative, and stimulate a musical response."

Over 200 poems are included in this Collection. They deal with the big issues of life – love, old age, war, jealousy, sadness, death, illness, the environment – in a way which can be both profound and moving. It is poetry which is often inspired and always evocative. It is hoped that this volume of poetry will bring to Ursula Vaughan Williams the recognition which she so richly deserves.

Stephen Connock
Chairman, Ralph Vaughan Williams Society

Contents

No Other Choice

(1941)

The Quarry

Along the green banks by the waterside
the fishers sit and idle summer through,
gazing at silver floats that nod and ride
above the gleaming cool where fishes slide
elusive under sky-reflecting blue.

Out on wide, frozen marshes speared with reeds
'til winter sunset the numbed fowlers lie
masking net and trap with rush and weeds,
waiting to lure some wanderer where it feeds
weary from flight across the snow-brimmed sky.

I'll sit a patient year to take a though
listen and wait until the bait is taken
and out of depth and height the creature's caught
and closed inside the cage of words I brought.
Then from this tranced wait and watch I waken

knowing that somewhere meaning goes astray,
once shut in language the essentials fade
like the heaped silver catch that lay
filling the angler's basket at the end of day
or the limp spoils of the fowler's trade.

Under the summer bank smooth water lies
where fish are flickering between reed and stone.
Brown winter sleeps beneath its icy skies
and high as cloud or wind the migrant flies
remote as thought whose words are still unknown.

Mountaineer

High, alone in this desolate world of the winds
where clouds quiescent lie on hills below,
I watch the ice, that like a girdle binds
the still white beauty of the mountain snow,
and shadows burn blue flame in each crevasse.
The afternoon streams slowly by, and night
follows that yellow hour, when mass on mass
the hills below stream to the plain in light.

The Naturalist

Solitude's life for you, the marvelling eye
accepting all it sees, and seeing all.
Where we go blind with hope, or lost in memory,
you listen till the intonation of a call
tells you of hunger, fear, or deep content
of busy creatures, earth dwelling and small.
Wing spread, wing shadow, beaks so curved or bent
name the bird to you, dappled markings tell
the moth, faint tracks the way an otter went.
To me an empty world, to you a spell
so deeply laid, that you are firmly bound
by sight and hearing, taste and touch and smell
to loved and living ground.

That thoughts are a continual surprise

Thoughts breaking like ridged waves
out of the unknown darkness of the mind,
a moment all the substance is displayed
and just as fast withdrawn, and left to find
only some small shells lying on the sand
and cold spray salty in an open hand.

As secret as the wind, wider than sky,
shut in this skull, my mind will lie
and let thoughts break like waves until I die,
as waves, slip through the hands
leave but a curled trace on the sands
and so return to their deep secrecy.

The Enchantment

There is no refuge while the senses live,
so you shall grow at last into a tree;
then, to the earth your autumn leaves will give
colours that shall return, in flowers for me.
So thought shall end, and, unafraid of chance,
instinct will shed your leaves or open buds each day.
You will need nothing then, you need not dance
to find an ecstasy, nor read nor pray,
but self-sufficient shall your branches spread
increasing splendour, deep between earth and stone
your roots find comfort; and then it shall be said
'how beautiful a tree has Daphne grown.'

Aloe

(The plant that flowers once
in a hundred years)

Seek and you shall find
no answer of music to the thought
or of colour to the sight;
knowledge is only bought.
Stone holds the form disguised
that you would bring to light,
and so we learn, surprised
that only in the mind
can the aloe flower
in half an hour.

The Gothic Angel

O those far staring eyes
that seem to look with man's imprisoned sense
and more than mortal certainty, to find
wisdom's a planet native to the skies,
are stone, are blind.
It is the maker's searching and his impotence,
though to a sculptured beauty he has bound
his spirit's hope, and sureties of his mind,
and set them in the clouds, remote from quarried ground,
those eyes are stone, are blind.

The Archaeologists

Excavations by Moonlight

The moonlight spreading across the hill
sheds a reflected glow on the heaped-up chalk
that we dug to-day, and where you walk
a long black shadow moves like a pointed quill.
Many juniper bushes are crouching around the pit,
but the gleaming chalk has given up its dead,
small heaps of broken pottery, brown and red,
an antler shaped as a pick, and the skull that stares at it.

On Digging up a Skeleton

In this skeleton I cannot recognize
wise man or fool: yet had I seen
the quiet body lying in candle light,
having come too late to read the living eyes
I should have known the man that he had been
at sight.

Marked by the spirit and the burning mind,
flesh mirrors self with small disparity,
and face and hands show all life's habits clear.
Is individual then to flesh confined?
Only an outline of mortality
lies here.

The Burial Place

Here at our feet the treasures lie,
stillness of death informing stone and gold,
once honoured flesh the little dust they hold
so secretly.

And one day other men will find,
deep drifted in forgotten dust of years,
the words we made to cradle hope and tears,
to free, to bind.

After Fishing

The contemplative silence descends
like shadows lengthening darkness on the grass.
Enamelled leaf from leaf sharply divided
is in the stream repeated
when the last brilliance of the sunlight lends
gilding to colour, that as it shines will pass,
for day is ended.

Along the riverside mist rises,
and the cold smell of dew, of water at night,
drifts with a wind that stirs the hanging willows
along the water meadows,
till a white owl, flying low, surprises
crouched waterbirds that chatter in their fright;
repeated silence follows.

Sight

Within oneself deserts and mountains are,
cactus desolation and polar night,
landscapes electric blue becalmed on white,
till outward vision answer the inner sense
more absolute than shadow, as intense
as movement poised in stillness, and aware
of wings alive for flight.

Prologue

Flesh to this meeting moves,
aware and sensual,
threading between casual
moments and things, to loves
predestined by some choice
made with both mind and voice
but blindly . . ..

Mind, like a bird in air
or comet, scars with flight
the distance, in delight
to find such freedom there,
but will not stare behind
to trace the path we find
blindly.

'I am two fools I know
for loving, and for saying so . . .'

I

Seven o'clock: all night my heart has counted
yesterday's kisses over,
remembering yesterday morning, when I went as a lightfoot lover,
that now am hunted
by more love than I can bear.

II

But past is past, and will not come again.
I thought myself bound-free, secure from pain
of any other love than that I have,
no echo even met the love you gave,
and so it was till the last moment came
I caught your fire, and cannot staunch its flame.

III

Ah when will this long weary night have end?
When will my heart its load of trouble spend?
But empty hearts aren't lighter or more wise,
and sorrow shines, dark lanterns in the eyes.
There's a choice here, until we choose and go
the chosen way, neither of us will know
whether we're fools or not, though time will show.
Only the crying of the arms we know, and guess
the body's everlasting loneliness.

IV

The stars are netted in the branches high
where the wind stirs
soft leaves murmuring together, and the dry
leaves of firs.

Fall evening, fall all darkness on us here,
branches bend down,
close this blue midnight round us where
we drown.

V

There are no debts in love
when you discover
your own heart's all that matters,
your own heart that scatters
its folly everywhere,
and reads in the eyes of a lover
the thoughts it would find there.

VI

Closed in your arms, all peace possessing,
sleep, like darkness round us folding
heart and spirit you are holding,
complete beyond all longed for blessing.
Made whole at last, what should this peace inspire,
O phoenix, dreaming in a sleep of fire?

VI

Hands, give him all the measure of my love
surer than any word.
Eyes, be deep pools of truth, where he may see
a thought more whole than constancy.
Heart, in his keeping, be at rest and live
as music and silence meet and both are heard.

Night

I

When in my arms you lie
heavy with sleep
I am more content than a deep
green river between high banks moving certainly.
Seen in the water trees are dark against the sky,
the reflecting water flows past, and I, to sleep,
drowned in green water, happily, deep
in warmth, in sleep,
and you asleep in my arms, contented lie.

II

Beauty, that rare and migrant bird,
has spread its wings round me to-night
alone and quiet in the candle light.
Why did you go? the night is still
the half moon lightens all the hill
and patterns leaves across my feet.
O sad that we can never meet
here in this moment, between light
of moon and candle, both burn and are obscured,
and beauty is a rare and migrant bird.

'Old wives a-sunning sit . . .'

Time's not an enemy to friends,
though words that kindle words grow less
and changed the tenses.
But kindness lingers in the deadening senses
and nothing ends,
though two that talked all night until the day
will sit together with no words to say
in easy silences.

The Changed Landscape

I remember a time
when this was a hayfield,
simple and pastoral as a nursery rhyme.
But since they planted pines,
and the trees have grown tall
in dark straight lines,
the simple flowers have gone.
It is dark under the branches,
I am afraid to walk here alone.

This girl is dead

(From the French of Paul Fort)

This girl is dead, she died at break of day,
this girl is dead, dead while with love she lay.
They lay her down alone, alone in her array
they lay her down alone, shrouded alone to stay.
They have come back to the fields, the fields at break of day,
they have come singing gaily, like any other day.

Lazarus

We waited in the quivering heat for his return.
None of us had seen a miracle before, but we believed
in the man, and his accredited acts. We were not deceived:
he did return.

We had thought, simply, that we should all rejoice,
gathering round him, strangely unchanged by the days
he had been dead in the dark, then go on our various ways
having heard his voice.

But when he came it seemed cold as night, and we fled,
having seen fear in his terrible eyes, and great despair.
We could not break into his isolation, nor did we dare
hear what he said.

But his sisters stayed unguessing, being blinded by joy,
they took his hands and kissed them, and led him inside.
In a day or two they forgot he had ever died
or had changed since he was a boy.

The Swans

Place.

The sea is bound in ice, grey, white and grey,
where the wide stillness holds no hope of spring
and light's a measure shorter than the day,
and cold is part of stillness: winds that bring
the snow are here imprisoned and must stay
frozen to earth, powerless to blow away
the lightest feather cast from a migrant's wing.

Here the swans gathered, resting after flight,
but from this desolation they are gone.
When the late morning touched their wings with light
they vanished southwards. When the winter's done
they will rest here returning, but till then no sight,
no sound will break this still unshadowed white
where the pent wind and prisoned wave are one.

Lullaby.

Listen, listen . . . the snow is falling
hushing sound in whiteness,
brushing grey glass lightly as a feather,
listen, listen, falling feathers heaped in lightness
measure the winter out in this white weather.
All the swans have flown together,
high above snow they fled in brightness,
soft as feathers snow is falling,
listen, listen . . .

Elegy.

Now they will lie till the unpitying spring
looses the ice and snow, sinew and bone,
and sweeps white feathers from each outstretched wing,
the swans are gone.

The dying swans who sing, who sing to Death,
a song ascending as their wings are stilled,
till earth at the last flutter of their breath
is echo filled

have lived to the full measure of their flight.
But these were netted where they came to rest
tired from the icy air: the colder night
froze on each breast.

Here, in the world abiding, beauty lies:
for unguessed pain, life broken, not a word,
only the legendary death, the visionary eyes,
the singing bird.

Alms

Sorrow, be metal for the mind of man,
not like white transience of the winter frost
that binds in pain forgotten soon as lost,
but to endure, as furnaced metal can.
Let the racked body and remembering mind
in some long lasting form their passion show.
Sorrow defend us, for us seek and find
hope to transform the blinded face of grief,
that from a thorn a flowering tree may grow,
the hurt give alms, the unwounded take relief.

To the Historians

Can you, with clear and practised vision
see beyond cities that will be destroyed?
or hear, louder than guns' derision,
a future freedom singing in the void
sprung from a war's decision?

We, urgent to know our hopes returning,
fear broken body and the desolate town.
How should we guess, beyond a city burning,
a harvest springing from the grass cut down
not singed and brown?

Death holds a mirror to distort our sight,
pain excludes wonder, grief dulls the eager mind.
Where do we follow? Migrant birds in flight
have never seen the lands they surely find:
blind lead the blind.

Soliloquy

Still in the valleys the echoes cry aloud
after my heart among these silences,
echoes of footsteps and shadows of palaces,
pearls in the water, mirrored towers white and proud,
and green branches.

Now I must learn the customs of solitude
An eagle's shadow flies along the ground,
the pillared clouds crumble without a sound,
no trees speak to the wind with the voice of a multitude.
What have I found?

I have found hills where sand and rock and time
become each other, build and disintegrate,
endless mutations of their primal state
in colours of desert and shadow, lava, fireopal, lime,
dark shale and slate.

Look from this height by moonlight – down and far
the world's rim curves no boundary to space,
the mountain's shadow darkens all earth's face,
and out beyond burns star and further star
I cannot trace.

And so they burned before the waters fell,
mist, dew and rivers filled the earth's deep sea
whence life rose winged and growing; ancestry
common to men and dragon. Bird, fish and animal
share mystery.

The past, all future then, from darkness came
as rivers rise from earth, and wandering find
a final sea, so journeys all mankind,
hopeful or fearful, wise man or fool, their journey is the same;
man travels blind.

Careless of us they made their living world:
thoughtful for us, some, with bequeathing hands
left wiser laws to rule their conquered lands;
for merchandise, for islands, in vision their ships sailed,
their buildings stand.

With time's wrecked shins and effigies of queens,
past days and hours unalterable lie,
and heir to all the past, I, living, cry:
'Spend all the heart's possessions, until Time quench
    the daylight green
in memory.'

Love in its brilliance and its desolation
is like the dancer's music, lovers are bound
within their passion; lost while music's sound
masks all the world beyond as stage and decoration,
a dancing ground.

They are the living, full of resurrection,
the lanterns set wherein the flames are bright,
illumination and surrounding night. . . .
two worlds alive together. What life springs from destruction?
What dark from light?

Waves that have strangled and drowned will never cease,
and fire forever blackens flesh with pain,
mirage of suffering builds each scene again,
the merciless imagination tormented turns from peace,
repeating pain.

But when there's no choice left, no chance to save,
strength matches pain, courage beyond despair
looks through the mastered flesh death will not spare,
but looks not back to comfort us, whose flame, the breaking
    wave,
or the beast's lair,

Or in stillness, alone without respite,
who can look back to comfort when the past
is all resolved? When sight is clear at last
for morning, or more darkness than depth of any tidal sea
where light is lost.

Now turns to never, the climber's empty hand
leaves the last hold, and clear his shadow lies
like a long track known to both heart and eyes
through time and place, by wood and water, harvest and
        barren land
whence echo cries.

Fall of Leaf

(1943)

Finding

Stranger to silence, listen, be comforted,
for sound and silence, daily interspaced,
meet here in sight.
Colour and sound are muted both by night:
bird after bird ceases from song and flight,
still, blue and deep,
distance outstretches to the sky, and shadows steep
in quiet the trees and grass, all houses, dark with sleep.
See and be comforted.

Here all past summers lie. Here their increase
spreads wider branches. Though they only lease
a lifetime's beauty,
time cannot touch the human memory
that flowers in you, lights for your living eye
known and unknown,
until you too, listening, have grown
one with the silence of all summers done
in the night's peace.

Looking back

The past possessed and bound in stone Lot's wife:
Orpheus turned back to a dead love from life.
And I look back, for both of these am I
and on the future their dark shadows lie.

Lot's Wife

If I turn back to stare upon the flames,
it is because the city, in my mind,
still holds my home, my days. The names
of square and street and garden still I find
conjure the place into sight's memory
till I am sure of their reality.

It is like this after a journey's done;
when one comes home and shuts the door
thinking of places left behind, the sun
still shines on them though left a week before,
and still the petals scattered on the grass
lie, as if days remembered never pass.

Reality is here; is the wind
that blows a smell of fire across our way;
it is the stones with which our way is lined;
the dust that chokes the tears, turns grey
the dark smooth hair: sorrow would turn it white
for grief is frozen; here's but a fool in flight.

To go, one takes provision for some days,
thinks first in terms of food and covering,
maps for the journey, choosing less known ways,
and small and special treasures that will bring
a thought of home into some far strange room
now waiting empty as an emperor's tomb.

Then we are gone. Turn at the corner, see
for the last time that curtain blowing white.
Part with a wrench from domesticity,
the copper saucepans that were always bright,
the linen piled and smooth with years to wear,
and cupboards filled, and flowers everywhere.

Sunlight half filled my room, and in my glass
behind my face, the shadow of a vine
traced its carved leaves, and there I was
a woman still. All that I saw was mine,
and like my tree I too had roots and spread
a sheltering presence. Now I too am dead.

The city lies smouldering ash and dust.
In its destruction fell not only walls,
the skill of builders too; and then you must
think of the labourers. The city falls,
the architect's design as well as stone
breaks into rubble, and creation's gone.

My heart is with the women whose lost days
were spent embroidering curtain cloth and sheet,
men who worked silver in fantastic ways,
those who made sandals for the dancers' feet;
painters and gardeners, all the craft and skill
of hands that follow and translate man's will.

As real as the sunlight when we fled
the winter's snow will cover arch and stair,
till grass shall hide the city and its dead
and the doors opening on nothing-there,
and the black ashes of destruction,
the body that will seek no resurrection.

If I could turn and see the smoke still blown,
still rising from the cities of the plain,
stone tears would fall upon a face of stone,
my body know the ruined cities' pain.
If I could turn and see . . .
stone tears would fall.

Orpheus

Singer of life, whose voice confines us all
in the enchanted bondage of one sense,
Death will listen if you choose.
Use your power, none refuse
pleasure drawn out in fine threads of sound
beyond the limits of intelligence.
Sing to the twisted spirits underground
until your lover rise as flowers rise:

possess their hearing till they bless your eyes;
for if you cease
and look within her heart to find your peace,
again she dies.

. . . and I

This stone was grooved to fit a hand.
I hold it now by the same grasp
its maker knew.
I found it on the fresh ploughed land
where, till this year, wild grasses grew.
What flowering summers lie between
these furrows and that green,
those fingers and my clasp?

Guess at the maker's questioning
where future, beyond working hands
grew in his eyes.
What did he see? The chipped stones bring
so little knowledge to the wise;
yet this is my inheritance,
made by skill, found by chance,
here on this common land.

The stone is mine; his vision less
than Time, reaping his sowing still,
gathers and scatters.
But I look back to him and guess
the past and not the future matters:
what's now makes then; turn to the past
for prophecies that cast
their shadows on my will.

Once of one substance, man, fish, bird
went separate ways, chose earth and air,
water, not fire;
and for their separate lives they herd
in confines of their own desire,
accepting life and finding death;
none but man spends his breath
making words, making care.

From a lovely face take years
till simpler beauty shows again;
imagine youth.
So, take from earth the marks it wears
of man's long groping after truth,
his harvesting and granaries,
his roads and palaces,
and walls against his fears.

The animals make lair and den;
the birds inherit songs and die;
the silent fish
move in dark seas, again, again
repeating beauty; while men wish
and search to know, possess and find
Earth cannot hold this mind
that seeks infinity.

As if the choice were half in vain,
rejected fire with lightnings fills
man's thought and dreams.
His gods with fiery splendour reign,
like light their inspiration streams:
and from his dark imaginings
angels ascend, their wings
blaze beyond mortal hills.

Yet he is held and clothed and bound
by the long past all creatures share:
sinew and sense
still bind life to its chosen ground
and task; us with obedience.
My hand inherits all the past,
and, while the senses last,
this chipped flint that I found.

Procris

Procris is lying at the waterside,
the yellow flowers show spring, the grass is green,
before a gentle wind the thin trees lean
towards the rushes, the rushes to the tide.
She will not see
the green spring turn to summer, summer go
in a long golden dusk towards the snow,
with eyes so lit by love that everything
burned, flowed, grew, blossomed, moved on foot or wing
with the guessed rhythm of eternity.
All her hope and will
flowed from her unavailing
and she knew darkness, as her eyes know now
shut to the daylight, and despair prevailing
she saw no way to go.

I.

The Institution

'Ten thousand stood round me, yet I was alone . . .'

Gathered here, like swallows before migration,
the old and poor come without possessions,
sit on benches, idle in the sunlight.
Spent flesh is withering on their bones,
muscles contracting, heads bent with a weight of days
that will not pass unless sleep stays
to be a day's companion.
They, like the swallows, have left their summers behind:
their words in a hundred soliloquies remember
name and place, child and hope and summer,
gossip at doorways, faces at the window,
women who were themselves coming and going
each at the centre of some world built of small possessions.

Each from her world of having comes alone
to wear the anonymous garments of charity,
to sleep in narrow beds close to each other,
to wake to another day of waiting
though the swallows have gone already
across the bright autumn sea.

II.

The Fortune Teller

Three-coloured cards between us lying
to me are emblems. What to you,
who look at meaning as I look at colour?
Where are you searching? Days like treasure lie
heaped in your hands; I choose;
you see the common boundary of to-morrow fall.
The careless past will someday be completed:
is it completed now within your sight?
Bring back, like gold washed from fabulous rivers,
promise fulfilled and knowledge growing wise,
clues for the maze, prophecies for despair;
build me a city, guide me to a door,
for this the cards are scattered on the floor.
What do you see?

Spider

Out of herself the spider draws a thread
and runs from leaf to leaf to spread
traditional and intricate
the pattern of her web: makes her estate
upon the air.
She watches with a black unsleeping stare
her net spread in the currents and the tides of day
for winged prey.
Then, having fed,
she wraps the shrivelled bodies of the dead
bumble bee and bottle fly
in twists of web as delicate
as the unopened calyx of a flower.

There are voices

There are voices speaking to each other everywhere
across the silence. Sounds hurrying, meeting, parting,
words made for comfort, fear, expedience, chance,
voices heard for the last time, and echoes starting
that will repeat a phrase for ever in the heart.
So many words traversing silence, threading the air
netting me in their meaning and their care.

Although he looks beyond the cloud and light
a shipwrecked man is bounded by the sea,
waves spring and die across his field of sight.
So I listen, listen as he will stare,
I for your voice, and he remembering land
beyond the waves' inhuman and unchanging dance.

Valentines

I

Too early for the daisy or cherry stones to tell
if he loves me, or loves me not, or loves me far too well.
Too early for the knot grass to answer yes or no,
so what shall I do till the daisies grow?
What shall I do till the cherry's red
to know if he'll ever say the things he's never said?

Why wait for the cherry? the buds are hardly green.
Why ask the daisy petals to guess what he may mean?
Ask him, St. Valentine, ask him to tell
if he loves me, or loves me not, or loves me far too well.

II

Women will always wear their beauty for you,
whatever they have, like a rose in the hair
or a silver dress. They will move like dancers
between low burning candles and the first light of day.
You will see the smiles caught in a dark mirror,
a scarlet shoe on the stairway, a footprint on the grass,
but not the living creatures as they pass.

This curl, this silver shoe, this rose is mine,
but I am here inside the gay disguise.
Find me, find me . . . the rustle of stiff silk,
masked laughter, thin hands with emerald rings and yellow fans
hide me from you. Love is more mad than blind
when masks and shadows are all that he can find.

III

Tipped with gold or sharpened lead,
with silver feathers for a wing,
Love's arrow curves through space to sing
quivering in the heart, and shed
there its wealth of care and grief,
there its joy beyond belief.

Though the dart be lead or gold,
fledged with feathers of a dove
that shows your destiny in love,
like the pilgrim's staff, behold,
between the spearhead and the wing
leaves unfold and roses spring.

Tired

Sleep, and I'll be still as another sleeper
holding you in my arms, glad that you lie
so near at last.
This sheltering midnight is our meeting place,
no passion or despair or hope divide
me from your side.
I shall remember firelight on your sleeping face,
I shall remember shadows growing deeper
as the fire fell to ashes and the minutes passed.

The Effigies

Who in their senses would envy the effigies?
Who, stepping from bright and coloured day
into this monochrome of dark and grey,
holding the summer's flowers, would be here and stay,
envying the crusader where he lies,
or wish to change this coloured silk for smooth stone draperies?
Each statue holds a truce with time. Time-fearing love
might easily ask no more than this unchanging state,
carved of one stone to be together and disparate
while centuries across horizons move.
O hope unknown
to share the unread inscription and forgotten date,
the formal gesture of prayer, the silence of stone.

There must be time for grief

There must be time for grief:
work has its hours, and love, food and sleep
take their due, and days go by
measured by necessity.

Drawn curtains show the morning,
the clock pointing the cue for entrance into day;
the dance has started, the dancer cannot stay:
the intricate discipline is beginning,
the sun burns time away.

Close the curtains, shut out night.
All day, all day
grief has eluded, darkened the corners of the mind,
edged a word, shadowed a hand.
If there was time to receive it I might understand,
might look into it as a mirror: in its reflection find
that the past recalls its love, is somewhere, whole and secure,
as travellers' cities, never revisited, remain
just as they were before.

But it is night again,
and it is sleep that takes my hand.
To-morrow there must be time enough for grief.

Fearing Apparitions

Why fear a ghost, shrink from a night of dreams?
Neither is what you knew:
or, if the shadow of the thing it seems,
it will be only gentleness to you.

My part of death

I

Words spoken lightly, words used every day,
familiar currency of touch and look,
so much belonging, familiar and expected,
has come to an end. I or any one else can say
the same things over again. You never may.
What have I heard and remembered? what neglected?
Searching the past for you, I look
at so many places, so many moods together,
the action flowing towards this brink, this break, this going away.

Death has so many powers I did not guess:
changing to-day, filling the past with strangeness,
making it more than it was, and the present less.
This is the water of petrification, flowing and turning to stone,
binding the past in a stillness I never suspected;
your words and gestures become unchanging, everlasting,
Stranger that was well known.

II

The houses we lived in are haunted more than remembered.
If I stood at a window surely I should see
both of us living there still, sitting in firelight;
moving, flickering flames lighting yellow walls,
warming tables and chairs, the colour of my dress,
pointing your heavy ring with flame; our idleness
full of content.
And I, the watcher outside, could not doubt the night
enclosed in the walls, in the past's serenity,
but would question my flesh and blood, not memory.

Which is the ghost? Had you or I looked out
from the warmth of then into the night,
would we have seen me curious and alone
looking through empty windows, and known
ourselves but shadows left inside a room?

So you are everywhere we ever went.
A word, a look, a quarrel all remain
bound to the road, the room, the well-known lane;
and I too listen, answer, quarrel all again,
and find our lives scattered across the south.

III

I've seen from flight at evening, small between earth and sky
horizons change from land to breakers everywhere,
the valleys narrow and the hills grow small,
the prehistoric track, the roman wall,
shadows of trees and towns diminish.
Our journeys, ventures, idlenesses crowd
into a smaller space, grow less and vanish,
for Time's wings drive me though I backward stare.

IV

Time's measured for the eyes by day and night,
the changing moon, harvest and hour-glass,
flocks of small birds gathering for flight,
bonfires and heathfires, and the glow-worm's light,
leaves growing dark and shady, frost that can surpass
the leafiest summer with white shadowing white.
Four other senses share the world with sight
watching the seasons pass, and centuries pass.
Year after year I shall hear wind and rain,
touch petals fallen from the almond tree,
walk in the snow, or shelter under leaves
while distance grows between us. No harvest sheaves
will turn green in my hand, be seed again,
nor sun stand in the sky because of me.

V

Though the newborn have all custom and usage to learn,
they hold, like the seed of corn, the fruit of trees,
promise and fulfilment. They inherit
all man's dependence on the earth and seas,
the journeys and the trophies of the spirit.
The newborn are sheltered by pity and tenderness;
who can comfort the dead, be gentle to them in their strangeness?
It is the living who learn
that earth makes individual ashes earth.

VI

Where shall I find the resurrection?
All the ceremonies for the dead
are paid in the currency of life,
the silver coin, stone jar and hunting knife,
folded draperies, wafer of bread,
the dirge and promise of the requiem.

The metaphors for death are night and sleep,
as if the ashes were scattered seed
sown in autumn for the future's need
and not for earth to dissipate and keep.

The dirge and promise of the requiem
stands between us and the dead, who are unknown,
who are strangers, having left all that we knew them by.
Is the seed barren? or what flower has grown?
Where shall I find the resurrection?

VII

We could have been old together,
argument stilled to tolerance, and content
grown a deep root from which our days would spring.
Trees grown for centuries together
have branches interlaced in long consent
where the birds stay to sing.
The separate branches make a shade together
and when the summer is spent
the leaves fall one on the other as coloured as the spring.

Firewatching

Moment, my certainty, where all the senses live,
sand runs so quietly through the hour-glass,
how shall this grain be held?
What is the evidence added together to give
sharp contours to the moments as they pass?

To live now is to look back. Touch what you will,
cup, plate, fine silk or necessary bread,
a hundred histories are there, for still
we inherit more than living from the dead,
more than a shack upon a barren hill.

Small, in the shadow of the enormous past,
a man descending a mountain might look down
and stare across a continent; the vast
territories, the cornlands, forest and town:
he by the spring, at the edge of the snow could see
the river widen to its estuary.

But we at the river mouth, loitering by the quay
where ships come loaded from some foreign land
with corals and bright birds and pearls and mystery,
look outward still, touch with an eager hand
this evidence of more discovery.

Measure the mountains by man's sight,
the earth by journeys, and the sea
by voyages to where the unknown lies,
by common currency of day and night;
bring home into this moment history,
be harvesters my ears, my hands, my eyes.

II

The summer night stirs with the lightest wind.
I can remember summer nights like this,
when under my window branches stirred,
and the cold scent of flowering may and earth
made my hands grope for all spring's promises.
And nights when moonlight shone on rivers, and the bridges
circled the water with reflected arches:
we walked in the dew, and others walked there in dancing dresses
pale as white clematis and phlox by the water.

O landscapes with remembered figures.

The lightest wind stirs in the summer night,
the siren fades above the darkened windows,
and beams of searchlights wheel about the sky
searching for death among the constellations.

Brighter than stars and guided by calculations
as delicate as the mechanism of a clock,
shells burst; explosions echo to the ground,
we count the alternate flash and sound.

Here we are tented in the brilliance of disaster,
here falling walls and the thick dust of plaster
carry it downwards, downwards into comprehension,
measuring huge pinnacles of hate and fear
by inches of destruction in our sight.

III

A city is burned down, the streets are gone;
Familiar spires no longer soar above,
white in the morning, where starlings cluster
turn in a cloud to settle and come to rest
wing after wing rustling like leaves of trees
against each other on a summer night.
The trees are blackened by fire, the branches gone,
the ashes are heaped and white.

Travellers, though never in Time returning,
remember cities once known, remember by heart,
and so are the streets we knew remembered,
streets where we walk with our shadows,
where other ghosts once walked in meadows.
Our city is part
of the heart's landscape. Build as they will
till the new skyline's familiar, the old like a dream returning,
a city unlighted at night remains for us still.
But when we die, the last survivor gone,
then, in the ancient fields, it will lie ruined, alone.

IV

Here are the empty houses and the shuttered,
the ruins where the rosebay grows
through gorse and bramble on the cellar stairs:
the theatre where we watched the acrobats
swing in the arc lights above the arena,
they were dancers, like moths in lamplight, feathers in the air.
And now the siren strings its web of sound over the city
fading away, and further warnings crying
silver and faint for miles and distant miles
from street to street, all across the country,
across the continents.
You cannot hear where the sound ends,
or know where there's a boundary to fear.

V

Fear has a thousand different forms and faces,
a devil mask for every eye
that stares from the empty place on the pillow,
or is heard in footsteps hurrying by
from unknown places in the night to unknown places.
There's no propitiation that can change
this hour to day, bring morning near
to count for one more day all that is loved.
Now is for ever to those whose hope is fear,
and sleep and daylight distant and as strange
as resurrection.

VI

Nothing is itself alone: the child that held a shell
wondering at the smooth and midnight blue
tapering to grey, and saw for the first time
the shallow curling edge of the incoming tide,
saw all his summers in the advancing waves
by all the seashores he would ever find
as certainly as memory can return
to those long tamarisk-shadowed days,
sea-sounding nights that held the child sleeping.

Though Here and Now are fetters to the limbs,
Now is ephemeral and will be lost
between this breath, this heartbeat, and the next;
and Here's not mine, but territory shared
with all the past and all to come hereafter.
A Roman helmet and a burnt-out plane,
with my lost ear-ring and the child's shell,
are silt in the river, dust on a buried hearth:
so stars still seen, symbols of constancy
thinned out to ash and vanished long ago
although their brightness still pierces our nights.
Destruction bears its long inheritance of weeping.

VII

Remember the legend of Adam under the tree of knowledge
that was man's shelter by day, where he watched the stars
through the bare branches in the winter solstice,
and followed the arch of the branches to make a bridge,
and gathered the fallen leaves to clothe his nakedness.
We have cut down the trees and squared the branches
and built a city from the sapless wood.
How should we, in our generation have understood
what Adam knew with the stolen fruit in his hand?

Need for Speech

(1948)

Need for Speech

Joy needs no words, larks singing over meadows,
swallows at evening, dipping from sun to shadows
touching the water's stillness under willows,
all peace and all content are clothed in light
closed in the crystal globe of sight.

A prisoner's anguish teaches his hand to write
scratched on the dungeon walls, or on the night
the words cut from his heart are diamond bright;
brighter than life lie his remembered meadows
and quieter than sleep the shadows.

The Old Actress

She's the fantastic princess of her dream,
round her bent shoulders there's a threadbare coat,
an agate brooch means jewels at her throat.
The waters of the moat that rock and gleam
where boats and swans drift on a captive stream
that keeps the world away, her pension can provide,
shillings and pence the silver-copper tide.
Her dyed red hair, her thin yellow face
nodding above the fire, still bright
where flames lend her rusty curls their grace,
are withered colours of brocade and lace.
On the floor a maze of beetles crawl,
embroidered dragons on a palace wall
could never glare so, stare so, flicker, run,
as in this cellar darkened from the sun.
Sitting alone I see her, but she's not alone,
she's dancing with two ghosts, Flattery, and Success,
with death perhaps three dancing steps away.
Her clock shows morning at the end of day,
six hours late it ticks with measured pace
like high-heeled footsteps in the paths of space.
The tattered firelight has almost gone
and darkness lies like velvet on her dress.

A boy dreams of birds

(for Johannes)

A boy dreams of birds
till they float above his head,
wings canopy his bed,
brush his fingers and knees,
garlanding trees
grown between dark and light
where horizons of morning spread
to receive their flight:

while he kneels by a pool
where swans with folded wings
listen as he sings,
curved necks bent to his hand
outflowering from land
fingers curved to a shell.
Here he can understand
all he must tell.

'Cold symmetric wings,
warm breast, my silver dove
never flutter or move
from hand or dream;
dark room, still seem
my wing-leaved grove
by a swan-shadowed stream,
no day cage my birds.'

The Peasant at her Window

She sits by her window listening with folded hands
while village sounds gather like swallows under eaves:
children play where a water trough stands
shadowed by fig trees; a boy with a bunch of leaves
drives cows in from meadows, cow bells ringing;
women call to each other from their open doors,
brown hay-makers ride home on the high hay-load singing,
and perpetual river murmurs to its shores.

She sits in age's stillness, orchard stillness,
the yellow ripeness of September days,
while evening turns to shadows, there she stays
her square brown hands learning their idleness.

Penelope

Certain parting does not wait its hour
for separation; too soon the shadow lies
upon the heart and chokes the voice, its power
drives on the minutes, it implies
to-morrow while to-day's still here.

They sat by firelight and his shadow fell
for the last time she thought, black patterning gold
sharp on the firelit wall. So, to compel
the evening to outlast the mornings cold
dawn by the quayside and the unshed tears,

she took a charred twig from the hearth and drew
the outline of his shadow on the wall.
'These were his features, this the hand I knew.'
She heard her voice saying the words through all
the future days of solitude and fear.

Wilders

I

The cottage stands alone
on a high pebble bank,
greenly overgrown
where brambles rank on rank
beat against the door
trying to go in:
and brown spiders spin
elaborate curtains that fall
grey on the blackened wall
while grasses creep through the floor.

The garden has grown wild,
its flowers revert
and are reconciled
with feathered weeds that skirt
the broken wall.
Bent fruit trees stand
in this no-man's land
knee deep in hay,
wind blows the seeds away,
and apples lie where they fall.

II

This is a quiet stretch of river land
where streams divide pastures, ditches are never dry,
where herons nest in willows and stand
waiting in shallows and pools all day for fishes
and cattle doze among flowering rushes.

This is a quiet stretch of time, an idle day:
watching is living, slow hours flow by
bringing content, carrying away
only silver ripples, cloud shadows on water
or a heron's feather, the colour of pewter.

III

To go inside the ivy-guarded door,
sit on stairs, climb to the upper floor,
to count the four small rooms and wonder
who lived here before,
is to long to stay, to shelter for ever under
this slated roof, listen night and day
to sighing branches, flowing river
that carries time away.

The hearth remains, sign of man's possession:
fire, burn to-night, welcome my succession;
shadows move where only darkness came
since dispossession.

I celebrate home-coming with a flame,
for man returns to where he lived before,
articulate sound shall measure the green silence
and sleep space day from day.

IV

All night trees mutter to each other,
dark yew to ash, sweet walnut to spiced bay,
codlin apple, bird cherry and near against the wall;
leaves rustle and stir, bindweeds smother,
thorns tear darkness, branches sway
to a gusty wind that eddies as water eddies
restless, restless, brushing sleep away.

All night the house speaks to itself, or me,
mortar flakes between bricks, falls on the splintering floor,
nails loosen in window frames where briony tendrils sprawl,
the hearth quenched the fire that only burnt sombrely:
rain should have climbed the stairs, wind unlatched the door,
or time let in sky and weather, forgetting
that man was tenant here before.

V

Go, no place remains
for man's pains,
for fire or hearth,
or ordered path;
plaster from lath
must fall.

Go, who comes shall find
the windows blind.
The roof tumbles,
the wall crumbles,
nettles and brambles
cover all.

Go, the walls shall soon,
like a cocoon,
break to release
the prisoned space;
and the lost green peace recall.

VI

Morning lies golden on thick dewy grasses,
herons fish for ever
in pools of silver,
willows stand with their roots in shadow,
cattle graze in the ample meadow
where mushrooms lie as white as stones.

Briar and bramble have entered the house,
climbing briony
outstrips dark ivy,
walls are trellised with bindweed and creeper,
trees are closer, silence deeper
and I shall go as the others have gone.

Jess

A mile beyond the road Ash Corner lies,
a lane leads to it, downhill, through the woods
where the young trees are barely shoulder height;
under them, in the spring, primroses light
the hellebores' dark leaves and cool green hoods
bowed over windflowers, cold as winter skies.

Jess lived enclosed by woods, by bird's-eye panes,
closed in the green shade of a rainy spring
when the rain drips all day from eaves and sills,
drips from the tasselled chestnut flowers and spills
into the hollow tulip leaves, while everything
grows thick and rank in gardens, fields and lanes.

All afternoon in her tree-darkened room
she danced between the mirror and the fire,
her shadow large and her reflection small;
she watched them both keep measure on the wall
moving as if they knew she would not tire
remembering music in the firelit gloom.

She danced alone because she longed to be
where others danced: because she could not read
or sew or daydream being filled with discontent.
She must outstrip the day, dance the unspent
hunger of her heart away; because her need
drove her lightfooted onward, where she could not see.

'Solitariness and my hurrying thoughts
meet and be one; accept this way of living,
learn satisfaction from enchanted sight,
let cold snow crystals and the globe of night
pattern tranquillity, so forgiving
this anguish of the creature trapped and caught.

I am self-trapped, so for what capture grieve?
I came here gladly, where else should I stay
but in a husband's home? and yet when he is near
there's nothing more to say. He is still dear
but separation grows in us. From day to day
we cherish tenderness in which we half believe.

Or is it idleness that saps my mind?
No: these rooms shall answer for my care,
our garden shows the work of busy hands;
but discontent twists dark and heavy strands
into the pattern of this life I share,
in which I walk as if dull, dumb and blind.'

Her intricate dancing steps cannot outwit
her heart's despair or the slow afternoon.
Rain falls silently, roof gutters run with streams
and drip perpetually. A broken bird's egg gleams
enamel blue on earth; the yellow cat called Moon
puffs out his fur and goes to sniff at it.

The door bell broke her thoughts, so she could run
to welcome someone, postman, country neighbour,
a voice at least, a break in heaviness:
she darted through the house, glad that her yellow dress
would be for someone's eyes, opened the door
to all that sense and truth and reason shun.

A stranger who had lost his way stood there
asking to shelter from the rain;
he'd missed the short cut by the water meadows.
As he spoke his voice touched all the shadows
and drew them round him, even the heavy chain
behind the door shone, stripped of centuries' wear.

He watched her see this as he spoke. He said,
'No things ill-done cannot be smoothed away,
things used made new. A second chance is given
to those who'll trade with me. No bargains driven
but simple give and take; you choose another way
and pay my price. The starving must be fed.

The starving fed – with their own flesh indeed –
the sleepless rocked to sleep – in their own dreams –
the restless, dull, unhappy, made content
taught to turn back upon the way they went.
Time is my hour-glass, up or down it streams
following pleasure, satisfying need.'

She understood his offer, knew she'd cast
the shadow of her disappointed heart
on joy and tenderness so withering them.
She saw her life too clearly to condemn
more than herself from whom she could not part
knowing how present comes as sequel to the past.

'What have I done with life that I should be
ready to change all that was dear so easily?
what have I done with all my nights and days
to see them coldly, with a stranger's gaze?
how can I hold them, shrunk so utterly
from all they were when they were part of me?

Ready to change all known, change day to day,
quietness that should clothe old age
not bind me in frustration. Let me live
as I consider living, and I'll give
my immortality, a distant image
of unendurable continuity, away.'

Then suddenly the stranger seemed no more
than a chance passer sheltering from the rain,
and the rain ended as he turned to go.
A small mark on her wrist remained to show
he'd touched her there, marking the insane
bargain his, and sealed; her wish secure.

Look inwards or look downwards where a stream
flows, but leaves the water-darkened face
seeing its own reflection clear as glass;
gaze mirrored there to watch the water pass,
it mars no detail, touches no curl or lace
nor stirs the deep enclosed, enclosing dream.

A falling leaf can break reflection, show
the river bed before it shapes again,
lie lightly as enchantment on five senses,
or sound's brief pattern upon silences;
time's measured on eternity in vain;
beneath your mirrored eyes the waters flow.

II

Her yellow cat was her familiar
gazing at darkness with moon-glinting eyes,
gazing at her with calm indifference,
both animals, both without innocence,
held together by inescapable ties
the devil's gift, to each peculiar.

She learned the spells of change, to say,
'Go into hare.' The bones closed in her hands
and changed to white-flecked paws, meanwhile her sight
showed only monochrome, her feet were flight
across the downs to where the gallows stands
half rotted now, and silence haunts the day.

Hay-field grass, in June knee high,
to her, a hare, tossed overhead
with sorrel and campion, the cornfields' hem,
and fan-tail barley on its knotted stem,
sainfoin and clovers white and red
were patterned for her against the sky.

She was so secret, her husband walking late
through flowering lanes, where petals on the grass
are white as daisies for the moths to find,
was blind to her, hare-like, as she fled behind
a hedge of roses, waiting for him to pass,
or cat-like crouched and slipped beneath the gate.

She'd leave a sleeping shadow of herself in bed
and run, disguised, ways overhung by fear
to a nocturnal hunting in the wood,
where beasts accepted her although she understood
none of their customs, nor came near
any companionship with them that hunger led.

Midsummer night she came along
by cottages that held deep sleep within;
roses and phlox breathed sweetness to the night
and swifts still screamed in darting flight
so high their cries seemed thin
as flittering bats' cries: nightingales in song

filled the dark trees with sound:
and honeysuckles and rose-coloured stocks,
pale as each other, still smelt of the day.
A heavy mist showed where the river lay,
and from three parishes she heard the clocks
say midnight to the midnight world around.

A man was leaning, idle, on his garden gate,
awake to watch the magical short night
change dusk to moonlight, listening, to share
the world with beast and bird. He saw the hare,
called to her and she came. His touch was light.
'Enchanted hare, why do you walk so late?

So late, so centuries late?' he said.
'You are alone, no coven on the hill
dances midsummer eve into midsummer day,
the village has lost its witches. Time blows away
even enchantments: yet it has left you still
wandering among things long dead.

Come from the beast.' So he undid the spell
as tenderly as if he took her cloak,
and she became herself and questioning.
How had he known her? 'What hare stands listening
to a bird's song, then moves as if she woke
from visions?' He laughed. 'You do not do it well.'

He led her to a small and whitewashed room
red floored, with shelves of books and everywhere
notebooks and papers strewn and spread
on chairs and tables and the narrow bed;
he cleared them for her, sitting there
he told her of the race of witches and their doom.

'Listen,' he said, 'you have your mortal years,
you have your senses and your hands,
knowledge is your inheritance and love;
you have the means for all, and yet you rove
these necromantic pastures in forbidden lands,
be wise, go home again.' She heard in tears.

'No, nothing's mine,' she said, 'I cannot make
a pattern of life; the threads unwind,
find me unready, and I do not know
even which way my eager feet will go,
only they will not stay; my heart and mind
divergent seek, not knowing what to take.'

Yet as she spoke she knew the search was done,
the stranger's face was suddenly well known
as if they had been many years together.
The window showed grey of a pigeon's feather,
a cloudy daylight, the short night had grown
invisibly to morning as they sat alone.

Grey as a pigeon's feather, grey as glass
dew lay on briar, on gossamer, on leaf,
and showed deep footmarks as she ran.
An early rooster crowed; the year's full span
blessed heart and eyes: corn grew towards the sheaf,
flowers to their fruit, as if all promise came to pass.

III

Often she would take fruit and flowers and go
down to the cottage, stay to talk and listen,
drawn to the stranger, so drawn there again
that her feet knew the way by field and lane
as well as her own garden, and would hasten
to him as certainly as rivers flow.

As the summer's self she seemed to live,
loving him with her heart's full certainty,
as if come home at last, as if a door
opened on music where silence was before,
or blindness faded leaving eyes that see,
or folded hands learned the heart's power to give.

The usual pattern of the days went on
till after harvest, when the heavy trees
bowed with their fruit, baskets full of sloes
bullace and damsons, that last of summer goes
in ragged gold, while from last flowers last bees
fetch their faint autumn honey and are gone.

She gathered the apples, russet, margil,
and crabs and pippins, some to store
some to make jam, and quinces, pears,
till the profusion that the orchard wears
spread indoors, filled the shelves, lay on the floors
or in two rows along each window sill.

And in the orchard, dusk and cold
she knew a hundred Aprils lay
between his birthday and her death,
vistas of springs she wept beneath
because not one would flowering stay
to shelter them together, young or old.

'Love so possesses me, so gilds my blood
I move in radiance, with finger points of light
touch and make new all daily things.
How can bones cage these beating wings
that stir to splendour, wake to flight,
then fold to hush and brood?

How shall I live, and not live at his side?
and how go back to those past years that lie
familiar in his memory? If I grow old
my middle years, my youth, should so unfold
run backwards, find him, stay, till I
safe in his past knew nothing could divide.'

So her imagination journeyed back
driven by passion, creating places, days,
where she was always his companion
driving all question of division
into her mind's more subterranean ways
where jealousy was waiting like a rack.

At first his words, his face, his being near
withheld her from her power as a witch;
but love unanswered shook her like a leaf
and longing quickened all her half belief;
unravelling her future stitch by stitch
she made her spell in awe and faith and fear.

She thought by making her young body old
her spirit, matching it, would stand by his,
and, without living it, have lived his past;
and so, become his counterpart at last,
grown with his life, her heart enclosed in bliss,
should wear its green untouched by any cold.

She took her mirror to the hollow night;
one future lay behind in shuttered sleep –
her husband lost, her children unconceived –
and for a moment's thought of this she grieved.
Yet this loss freed her, there was no way to keen
this might-have-been, her love must travel light.

By witches will under the starry night
she made one moment carry years away,
and through the whirling sequence saw her face
shrivel and shrink and lose its summer grace,
a scrawl of purple veins stain her thin arm and stay,
her bracken coloured hair grow thin and white.

The devil's voice answered her anguished thought:
'Where can you go, taking the last steps only?
without the years achieved, what beauty grows?
count up your follies, think, what river flows
back to its source? My lovely, lonely
witch, fool, lover, running hare, see, you are caught,

snared in the power I gave you. In this spell
you grasped at things not yours; and now
empty, refusing, you are quite alone;
you should have lived all life, endured it to the bone,
taken its hours; for what have you to show
for seventy years that twenty could not tell?'

So morning came, with morning's busy sound,
cockcrow, and milk churns rattling at the farm,
an early wagon rolling down the lane.
She saw the silver-shining weather-vane,
she saw the golden bracelet on her arm,
she saw her mirror lying on the ground,

and walked toward the house uncertainly,
opened the door, drew back the curtains, spread
the breakfast cloth, wishing for yesterday,
touching familiar things, wondering what words to say,
because she heard her husband's heavy tread
she hid her face and waited desperately.

The Walk

You have given me autumn for ever and ever,
each leaf of October gold is mine,
pheasant-plumed plantations, fire-coloured beeches,
a living sky, a hill's unbroken line.

Year in, year out, as the season's pattern changes
sight will touch a sleeping memory
with a leaf, a colour, till it wakes and ranges
back to the clearest seen, longest remembered.

They've gathered and carted the very last of the sheaves,
gleaners gone, ploughing will soon begin,
and the hunter's moon will shine, gales blow all the leaves
in a whirl of yellow across the fields.

Nightfall nor snow nor winter equinox blowing
can touch this afternoon when all is still;
the heart has gathered its harvest, spring is fulfilled,
now is forever and autumn is this hill.

So, to its certainty . . .

Travel through all the latitudes of earth
the compass needle quivering on the dial
seeks its known centre, turns with every step,
sure of direction finds out magnetic north.

Hear the cool spiral curve and coral lip of shell
always murmuring with seas' unending sound
although it lies a century away
from the Pacific shore where it first fell.

So, to its certainty, the heart must turn
acknowledging no other resting place.
So from time-bounded love the word remains
singing cold echoes on the shores of space.

Winter

I

Arctic midsummer: dawns in light on light
across snow meadows where nothing grows to reap,
a shadowless world, a day that has no night,
a lidless eye that cannot close in sleep.
The long unpointed hours loiter there
holding the image of the risen sun,
brightness that shapes nothing gilds the air
from empty April till barren autumn's done.
This is an easy symbol as it stands;
add sure foreknowledge of the polar night,
eternities of darkness, shuttering hands
compelling blindness on the dazzled sight,
and all the frozen springs buried so deep
they cannot quicken into tears and weep.

II

Here's love, spent and unspent,
where shall it grow if not between your hands?
where shall it rest, if not at home with you?
where shall it wander, if it must be lost,
silence our only son, our pillow separation?
Go through the world, where people lean
out of their lives, out of a window
to speak to a stranger, to pity the unpityable,
asking 'who are you?' gentle and uncaring;
and 'whom am I?' the wanderer answers, staring.

Between our hands' close-folded fingers, time
flows like brightness streaming from a lamp.
Look in my eyes and find your mirror there,
I look in yours to find my desolation,
I look in yours and find my love unspent.

The Little Owl

Branches of ice cage in the winter here
while rain and dew are stayed in brittle light
and mirrored moons appear
silver reflections splintered into glass,
glittering like phosphorescent seas at night
whose shallows are the hoar-frost crested grass.

The silent house has eaves and sills of snow,
snow muffled windows; smoke flies above the thatch,
a width of yellow points the door below
where a shawled woman stands
calling a little owl, aching to watch
it starve beyond the kind reach of her hands.

It would not leave the angled chimney stack,
five days she watched it, clinging close and cold,
or, waking drew her curtain back
and heart sick, saw its sculptured feathers lying
closer against its breast, its wide eyes hold
points of starlight, brighter as more dying.

"Where's the lost language man could speak with bird?
How can life say to life – come, shelter here?
Will no look call, since there is no word
left to speak truce to war that man has made
on all wild creatures till his shadow's fear,
and even my hand stretched out makes you afraid?

O bird, have pity on my tenderness;
hunter, forgive trap's iron teeth and spring;
winged one, forget the caged, blind lark's distress;
our lives both grow from far-shared ancestry
and meet in need for winter sheltering,
I from cold earth, you from the frozen sky."

As easily tame midnight to the hand
as tame this fugitive small bird of prey.
It lay at morning with its wings wide-fanned
and feathers ruffled by the wind to show
their warm and russet touched with silver grey
soft as the feathery snow.

Spring Evening

Out in the cold March evening on the silver branches
the blackbird's song is clear in the clear light,
and curling hyacinth's in heavy bunches
crowd in the grass.
Now while the pointed buds wait for the sun
to spread their folded green;
now, when day's work is done,
while smokes of evening fires climb straight and blue
against bluer woods, I lean
on the window sill with idle hands,
watching pigeons ruffle, preen and run
while earth prepares for summer, man for night.

Noah's Ark

There was no presage of the coming rain
when the finished ark lay moored below the town.
On holidays the citizens came down
to see the ship, sails folded by the shrouds,
and water butts, and all the stores for grain,
and Noah watching for the thunder clouds.

A familiar landscape of wheatfields and flax
lay at the river's edge; pasturing herds knee-deep in grass
straying, while shepherds sang. At evening
haymakers and milkmaids came home with garlands.
Days, ordinary as other summer days, would pass,
stay, linger, so diminish into night,
stay, or vanish in memory or sight
till clouds gathered, till the rain began.

Now, with the thunder, in a sudden dark
as deluge breaks across the pastoral dream
the ship wakes, each rope, each beam,
gathers her strength, becomes a unity;
life's only shelter, the protecting ark
casts her moorings to the rising sea.

II

The rain is grey, the fields are flattened brown.
Sudden rivers lace the avenues
or batter on tall doorways in the town.

Soon water will strip branch and bedroom bare.
leaves tangle with gold mirrors in the wrack,
floods lap over the last marble stair.

Now take the perfect pattern of the kind,
two of each species and no more, no more:
to outstretched hands, beseeching eyes, be blind.

Gather life's safety: here burns the only light,
here is the heart of all creation's limbs,
the only swiftness and the only flight.

Long seasons shall surround you still with rain,
moon's longer tides draw out an endless sea,
nothing promise any land again.

Hope gives a morning when the mist will break
to show a mountain-top whence waters ebb,
a flowering island, where dayspring shall wake . . .

but trust no compass, even the steady north
offers no safety now, the sky no star,
and no known harbour waits this setting forth.

III

It could be night for ever
lost between earth and sky,
mountains and islands lie foundered far beneath
where boiling whirlpools threaten 'never, never,
shall any morning break but death
on tattered sails set for eternity.'

They listen, listen, within
as lamplight rocks and sways,
each one enclosed in separate memory
or crying to time 'when will a world begin?'
Each thought a century,
while hours grope toward completed days.

It could be night for ever
where colonnades of rain
march endlessly across unending waves,
footsteps repeating 'never, never, never,'
while a wind veers and drives
white sea-crests faster round the world again.

IV

Brood, brood upon the waters, sudden peace.
Silence lies gentler than rain,
breaking clouds reveal a moon again
promise and certainty that night will cease.

Morning landfall ends captivity.
Fly freed my raven, fly, my shining dove,
from the imprisoning shelter of my love
spread wings against a rainbow sky.

Go now my children to your waiting land,
mouse, weasel, fox and spider, moth and bee,
lion, leopard, unicorn, go free,
as Adam named you, I bless each with my hand.

Here, on the future, is your anchor cast.
Go, and so multiply that air will fill with song,
jungles with strength; each go where you belong.
Only man's memory turns toward the past.

V

When all the animals had gone away
the empty ark lay beached and derelict
but sheltered humans still, by night and day.

Two daughters, murmuring, spoke of household things,
'Remember, sister, custom and custom's use,
from what tradition all our usage springs.'

'But when plants grow, will we know each by name,
for wine or balm or fibrous thread to spin?
We knew the total, but not whence it came.

We knew the pattern, each thing by cost and due,
our scope was understood; here we must discover
from what wild elements that order grew.'

Sunset flared across the desolate miles
touching bare trees, matted sedge and water,
turning cracked mud to fine golden tiles.

Then the third daughter, like a poppy, spread
her crimson veil and danced on golden feet;
and Noah blessed her beauty as he said:

'Her part is chosen, she shall sing and dance
remember legends and all names of flowers
and teach her children their inheritance.'

VI

Cold sighing waters of the flood recede,
rock slowly down to stem, to root of reed,
to silt beneath dark centuries.

Between kind elements of earth and air
water lay chained by shores, fire kept its lair
crouching on man's domestic hearth.

Man, life's image, made, marred, made again,
perpetual and ephemeral as grain,
grows to splendour, withers to despair.

While pinnioned flames strain from captivity
the heart affirms the phoenix cannot die,
but cold sense questions, 'who shall live?

Who will escape this time to live and grieve
over lost wisdom, and with love retrieve
all loss in new beginning,

as summer leaves its seed
shut in a berry, a bossed poppy head
from one flower scattering many?'

VII

Man stole a fire from the sun
built a hearth where it should burn
to shelter him with warmth and light.
Fire his fable and his truth
blazed from heaven to crown his mind,
while, in silver censers swung,
incense rises with his praise.
But the sultry winds of hell
blow through crannies of the heart
with the fears of fires to come.
Fire in heaven, fire in hell,
both his myth, both his dread,
underfoot and overhead
clasp him in predestined flame,
unleashing all the fires of earth
to dance with shadows at his death.

VIII

Man, have pity on man.
Rain from the outraged sky
drowned the innocent earth
yet the seed did not die.
Flowering from that rebirth,
man, have pity on man
as you hold the fire in your hand
that can destroy mankind
and desolate every land.
If the power and the glory is this,
a flame that burns to the bone,
what shall be left to grow
when you and your fires have gone?
What maimed and desolate few
shall recover life's full span
from among the ashes of time?
Man, have pity on man.

IX

In Noah's ark, in safe captivity
all perfection of creation lay.
Now, chance chosen, what will you inherit,
what ghosts shall live, rise from your memory?

No bird will bring leaves from a living tree
to you, unknown, who may survive the fires
and find by moonlit craters mirages of water
among the calcined bones of history.

Shall dry bones live? Or is our language lost,
last echoes of voices singing in Gothic aisles
beneath bright ramparts of eternity
a vision faded leaving only dust?

Take all from us that our doomed hands can give.
If all we built lies fallen, still remains
the skill we leave as dower and heritage
to wake and grow again in those who live.

So save us from annihilation,
remembering our legend, take our love,
evidence of our lives, surety for your own
motive and counterpoise of all creation.

World without Man

O all ye works of the Lord,
all that imagination could compass and possess,
to whom the exhortation was to praise and bless,
to inarticulate innocence
love must resign you now with every sense.

O light and darkness,
no longer measure of toil, shelter for sleep,
alternate hemispheres of day and night, you keep
pace with the seasons for which man's names have gone.
O fire and heat, burn for yourselves alone.

Rain, rivers, waters of the firmament,
the ships of history foundered in your tide.
Our derelict gardens by the waterside
flower in a waste of roses, shoulder high,
no sight will gather into memory.

O snow and frost,
no footsteps maze the whiteness, drifting deep
in clefts and valleys, glittering on the steep
sides of the hill where living beasts still range
unremembering how the seasons change.

O winds and stars,
music and words in silence are confounded;
known and unknown flow into the unbounded
state of being, where no comprehension
gropes for meaning, calculates dimension.

O all ye works of the Lord,
freed from man's legend, his instinct for salvation,
live: for the timeless morning of creation
aged only by man's measure. He has gone.
O sun and moon, burn for yourselves alone.

The Senses

Senses are the immeasurable I,
boundaries and gateways to the state of man,
separate and inseparable
as five arches of a bridge's span:
or as a consort of stringed instruments
allowing one voice a theme's authority
to hold, not break, the others' company.

Strangers, we wear the livery of earth,
impersonal grace given to each living thing,
shed in autumnal seasons to arise
and clothe fresh generations in the spring.
Trees that outlive men, man that outlives the birds,
flowers that live longer than the mayflies' day
touch past and present in their birth and death,
inherit all they are to give away.

Love marries us by every sense to earth,
creature in creature seeking perpetuation;
Myth is our child, in nature's image made,
to bear the burden of our adoration.
We have asked more than the natural dole
of root or wing, flower or bone's duration;
Possessed by thought our word's new boundaries
impose the heaven and hell of our creation.

Astronomers, from towering centuries,
watch constellations move in changing light;
wise in foretelling they know that life will die
and Time subside into a final night
where broken pillars of the alphabet
lie strewn across the desert's empty page,
leaving to silence and the winds of space
only the ruined fragments of man's age.

Sing, stars, that close your ranks in flame on man,
whose sight gave beauty to your radiance,
tradition knew the music of the spheres;
gather earth back into your endless dance.
Sing as you take life's ground again for death.
Man has no share in this captivity,
his spirit wakes, plumed with immortal wings,
set for his heart's assured eternity.

Wandering Pilgrimage

(1952)

Man makes delight his own

Man makes delight his own:
endless creation of his labouring days
captures for human terms all he has known.
From far-sown grain his gathered joy has grown
and, turned to sound or stone,
perpetual and unchanged for ever stays.

So, though he sleeps or dies,
his music wakes like Beauty from her night,
his words still cry his heart, for seeing eyes
his work declares how bright a landscape lies
untouched by centuries,
living beyond his perished, short delight.

The Headland

Along the coast line see the tides engrave
their contour lines in phosphorescent light
marking the rush of each incoming wave
and where the cliff foot breaks each arc of white.
Land juts above horizons of long clouds that lie
like further islands in a sea of sky.

Vision goes seaward: all the dark below
streams up the shore to storm the cliff and land
or rocks' tranquillity between an ebb and flow
leaving a line of plunder on the sand,
thin as an in-shore echo of the deep,
a wrack of dream along the edge of sleep.

Vision goes seaward: all the birds that fly
on their migrations, driven before the cold,
span in their voyage the same expanse as I,
seeing continent from continent unfold
as wave from wave rises with plume and crest,
white wings outspread and the white feathered breast.

As bird I fly to summer; and as rock I wait
endless and patient, pillar of the land,
victim of water, ceding my estate,
changing by grain and grain from stone to sand;
as woman, watch the wild birds' migrant range
and sea and land in their long interchange.

For herbs' lost magic and lost ritual charm,
made to compel the body's transformation,
leave us with only wish and thought to arm
the variable heart against time's devastation.
Grief can no longer change her tears to be
a spring that quenches thirst eternally.

Grief can no longer change her tears, no more
the hunted turn to fish or bird to share
these little silver pools along the shore
or the cool pastures of the upper air.
No roses mark where, separate, lovers lie
twining their white and red into one canopy.

Gamut of being, from life's humblest seeds,
that hold a harvest in their grain's confine,
to man's, with destiny of mighty deeds
or the traditional beauty of a line:
into predestined form the pattern flows
and grass, leviathan or prince so springs, so grows.

And subject to their bounds all creatures live
in separate kingdoms of the temporal world:
I may not turn to reed, nor as a laurel give
sweet shade from hands with all their leaves unfurled.
Yet I am woman, I am land and sea
housing this moment of eternity.

Vision goes seaward, sweeping like a wind
over blue meadows glittering to the light,
a wandering spirit, searching far to find
a summer ending to its winter flight,
a land spread wide with promise, filled with joy
dream that no truth can equal nor destroy,

where, beyond drought, beyond our famished days
the miraculous harvest stands for us to reap,
and rain has blessed it, and the sunlight stays
pent in each ear in heavy, golden sleep,
while afternoon in endless brooding peace
lies on these acres of the heart's increase.

So Moses stood alone with death upon the hill
watching the children of his care descend
to plentiful valleys, and heard their voices fill
the pass with echoes, and the echoes end.
Light died above the plains and stars lit all the air
above the inheritance he could not share.

So vision dies: from such a final height
looks down on kingdoms that it might have known,
along a coastline curving out of sight,
on the sky courses where the birds have flown,
yet is still one with bird and land and sea
housed in this moment of eternity.

The Siren

* And Uriel said to me: *'Here shall stand the angels that have lain with women . . . and the women they seduced shall become Sirens'.*

And if I sing
along these coral beaches till the caves
hold echoes murmuring
in every rise and fall of summer waves
clear as iris, curved as swallow's wing,
perfection to perfection answering,
it is of grief, a shadow of lost joy.
My silver tears fall from a ceaseless spring.

An angel, torn from heaven, defeated in the sky,
still lit by glory and still winged with flame,
in reckless beauty for the world to tame,
fell where my island basks on outspread sea,
by bastions of a city crowned with towers,
and terraced vineyards, tapestries of flowers,
down to blue valleys where my orchards lie.

Here mortal love was shelter for a day;
peace in my arms was healing for lost pride;
soon his light faded and his wings fell wide –
O wounded splendour journeying to death.
And even the memory of paradise
sank into silence, withered from deep eyes,
as like the shadowed moon he waned away.

But memory wears the blazon of his wing,
gathering me to limbs of fire and dew,
a birth of joy and grief wherein I knew
celestial language, voice of wind and star.
By light transfigured and by shadow slain
these are the songs of heaven I sing again,
mourning his beauty.
Mourning his beauty of my love I sing.

Singing I weep,
yet bright enchantment falls upon the sea
where the waves reap
their harvest of wrecked ships eternally,
for listening steersmen lose the course they keep,
forget the rocks and drown cold fathoms deep.
For none can share my joy or touch my grief.
I sing for ever and for ever weep.

* Enoch.
Quoted in *"The White Goddess"* by Robert Graves.

Magdalen

In a Pietà by Botticelli

Weep, your tears fall
upon his tearless eyes,
weep for the slain god pillowed on your knee
whose death acknowledges that he was mortal too:
lovely as love asleep he lies
and lost to you.

The others stand
separate in despair
learning the anguish of their broken hearts,
how far a journey can be made in grief,
how heavy is the sorrow that they bear
without relief.

But you have found,
holding his fallen head,
fingers may tell a tenderness unspoken.
Death, for this moment, gives him to your keeping:
For parting yet to come your tears are shed.
Now he lies sleeping.

Spoken to a Bronze Head

Bronze, where my curious fingers run
matching each muscle and each metal feature
with life's austerer structure of the bone,
each living plane and contour so well known,
you will endure beyond the span of nature,
be as you are now when our lives are done.

On unborn generations you will stare
with the same hollow eyes I touch and see,
look on a world in which no memories share
the living likeness of the face you wear,
keep, in unchanged serenity
all that time gave him in your guardian care.

His name is yours to keep, so will his glory be,
who are his only, his inheriting son:
and when the hand that writes so ardently
the sound of unknown sound reaches finality,
the music captured, all the work well done,
stand in his place and bravely wear his immortality.

The Bird Dream

It seems more like a memory than a dream,
the distant landscape lying blue and clear
empty of sound, no rumour, smoke or cry:
below, a gentle curve of flowing stream,
and overhead the birds sail far and near
a plumed white fleet cruising the cloudless sky.

I, with a few and shadowy strangers,
listening in silence through a summer day
hoping to hear some message or command,
knowing ourselves beset by unknown dangers
but nothing more, whether to go or stay,
unknown companions in an unknown land.

All we had left for food was country bread,
offered most gladly for the birds to share.
I went alone, knowing the gifts' full worth,
to scatter crumbs; their ritual feast outspread
I called on then as powers of the air,
I called on them speaking for the earth.

Out of the cool and furthest blue they came
turning and wheeling, circling to my feet,
their feathers shining, light as foam or lace,
white peacock birds with crests of crystal flame,
celestial creatures that bent proud heads to eat
the last food of the last of mortal race.

Now there was nothing left for hope or fear
no backward thought for what the way had been,
the last possession given without dismay,
passion, profusion, all were gathered here,
joy blazed through every sense and grew serene,
a flowing tide that bore all else away.

Then rising, rising up through veils of sleep,
through clouds and vapours, webs with points of dew,
half waking, half in dream, I grope for words
that I may have the world's-end hill to keep:
my eyes meet morning in the room I knew,
my heart still sees the flock of heavenly birds.

'Learn to love said nature, and leave all other learning'

Piers Plowman

Love, be my light, the sun to which I grow,
inform each word, be reason in each thought,
and life that burns within each seed I sow:

be the known aspect of world's time and space,
wisdom and innocence in equal rule
hemmed by the clear horizons of your grace.

Theme of life, compel and guide all less,
be word of power and summoning of sense
for all man's hope and wonder must express,

Love, in your power, let me be blessed and bless

'All things come alike to all'

Ecclesiastes 9, 2

I am life's vessel, knowing light
knowing the separate world of sleep,
between these hemispheres I poise,
my body the one globe they keep.

All early life, assured and young,
towards my mirror I would lean,
questioning my reflected eyes
Where is love? What will it mean?

For then all promise lay ahead,
a waiting forest, where the trees
would shelter joy with flowers and shade,
romance lie pillowed on my knees.

Tall avenue and tangled thicket
fell at a word, and all was light,
wonder from wonder, I was love,
a bird at zenith of its flight.

In this clear climate I have lived,
learning the tides and paths of air,
the famines and the thirsts of sky,
the heavy weight my wings must bear.

And now I lean upon the day
as once before my mirror's glass
learning as every one has learned
how quickly, quickly years will pass.

The forest closes close again
gathering mystery into green:
thickets lie violet deep in dew
under the branches' dark serene.

Where love was waiting for my life,
power familiar and strange,
death is his waiting counterpart,
I recognise their interchange.

See, see the cradling leaves of life,
cupped hands that open to the sun,
gathered the morning for their joy
and fold and fall when day is done.

To a 'Cellist

Centaur is man and stallion, gloriously
pasturing masterless on plains of air,
a merman wears his raiment of the sea
and sphinx takes all the desert for her lair:
part human creatures, in equal part still free
in the beasts' world that half their bodies share.
Musician, hand to bow grafted in mastery,
goes like an angel where no mortal dare.

Composite being, man's intelligence
and tautened strings on wooden shell, sets free
voice beyond speech or words' close boundary
to shape a world in logic of pure sense,
to comprehend beyond experience
silence and sound in measured harmony.

A Summer Story

I

Here land acknowledges surrounding sea,
trees crouch in shapes appointed by the wind,
sheltering banks half hide the wandering lanes
and houses are built low with one wall blind:
the little church stands against winter rains,
stands against sun and wind in tiny majesty,

named for a half-forgotten fairy Saint
who set his mark of magic on this place.
The gate hangs broken on a rusty hinge,
and shuttered windows, locked doors show no trace
of present use: all the wild hedge plants fringe
the unmown churchyard, growing without restraint.

In lulling silence here the landsman lies
who loved a mermaid. Sheltered inshore he sleeps
whose plough and pasture ran beside the sea
along the headland where the high tide creeps
into the caves, below the fields, where she
would sail to meet him and enchant his eyes.

He lies in lulling silence, that is made
of smallest sounds, for the bee comes and goes
and bird songs lace the light days of the spring,
and falling rain pearls petals of the rose;
the lizards rustle and the crickets sing
while summer leaves murmur in ample shade.

Learn from the blurred incision on the stone
only of birth and death; what flowed between,
passion or comfort, is sealed here untold
though village legend says that she was seen
weeping among the rocks when his bell tolled,
and round his name have many stories grown.

An only son, working his father's farm,
wise with the beasts and gentle with the land,
he grew contented in his world of day;
he had the strength of morning in his hand
and April beauty, golden, with eyes as grey
as the spring sea lying in waveless calm.

In blossom-heavy air one happy night
he walked through woods, and, for his seeing glance
the rising moon lit every frond and leaf
and every flower shone back her radiance,
spring's perfection, sudden, heart-breaking, brief,
kindled to magic in that opal night.

Too early for the nightingale, yet he heard
a sound that wrought all senses into one,
as if the scent of flowers had found a voice
woven with shadows, as if the moon had known
the music of the stars, and did like them, rejoice
and sang above the branches like a bird.

His heart was lost then, lost sky-high, sea-deep.
He called through thickets in the little wood:
no one was there to answer his wild words
where ash and cherry in their silence stood,
closed to his question, hiding all their birds
under a leafy canopy of sleep.

And all lay quiet on the empty moor;
he crossed the heather, his shadow ran beside
keeping his pace and mocking his despair
with larger gestures and its arms thrown wide.
He reached the cliff, climbed down its rocky stair
and stood alone on the cool, sandy shore.

The sea was shimmered with the moon's clear light
but as each wave rose up and curved to break
it turned to dark below a flashing mane.
'Voice', he cried, 'angel or spirit, wake
from sky or water, wake and sing again.'
His shadow too wept and implored the night.

Then curling water bore her to his side,
a tide of breakers was her retinue,
playing around her in a dancing throng,
and he, waist deep in seas, spoke as if words were new,
cried to her beauty, 'I waited my life long,
and if you had not come I must have died.'

'I am the water's self, of foam and light,
my beauty is a vision of your eyes,
my being, a chance of moonlight on the wave,
my voice, your echo of some paradise;
I am and am not: is there a man so brave
who would possess the sea and drown in night?'

'I would possess the sea if you are sea,
drown in the arms of night if they are yours.
What is possession? Is it to know? to take?
I know and give. Your sea had found its shores,
your night meets day at last and so must wake,
for love gives seeming its reality.

Before your music reached my inland sense
I walked the days in small simplicity
and there time's lesser boundaries hemmed my place,
now they are broken and my eyes can see
how small they crouched beneath the dome of space
where the stars cluster in vast brilliance.

What you have given you cannot recall:
if you are of myself, then I am whole.
If you are nothing O for me you live,
and in your being I have found a soul,
another sense: wisdom and joy you give:
yourself thus given, I am given all.'

As daylight came, as the slack water turned
from idling at the flood to full retreat
it bore her from him, carried her away
leaving him burdened with triumph and defeat:
morning lay cold on land where she'd not stay
but on her waves the dancing sunlight burned.

He walked home slowly; in each step retraced
he lived his search across the night again;
despair, then known had flowered to living grief,
joy, then half wakened, lit his dazzled brain;
nourished by both he went in sure belief
that spring had risen in his desert waste.

And she, once disembodied voice and wrack of storm,
composite memory of a thousand days,
a figure-head carved by a sailor's hand
skimming translucent calm of summer bays,
and drowned girls' beauty, captured from the land,
gathered all these into her single form.

So each of each created a new creature
and from each other made a new world wake
out of the substance that was there before
imposing on each other what each sought to take
a mirage or a vision without flaw
and earth wed sea against the use of nature.

II

Enchantment blows about a day, a place.
Return from far and it is always found
seeming to grow between the blades of grass
or lie like dew, unfading on the ground:
some moment, spent there once, can never pass
but leaves its blessing as enduring grace.

So was the cove in which they used to meet;
she sailed to him, in through an arching cave,
a doorway to the sea shadowy and deep
cut from living rock by living wave;
his way to her was down a path so steep
haste had taught him, and shod and winged his feet.

Lost all day long, only the visiting tide
strewing its-shells along the curve of sand
or streaming seawards knew that they were there
lapped in the thymy breezes from inland.
More lost by night when all the stars appear
to light their beauty lying side by side.

Safe while their language is still touch and sigh;
safe while their sight is bounded by desire;
safe while her arms are haven to his heart;
safe still, although he knows and marks the hour;
safe in the anguish that they know apart,
and safe while summer fills the hollow sky.

Each day the sun and land delighted share
the ripening harvest, turning it green, then gold,
from gold to palest ivory, bleached and bright;
and down the hedges the calendar is told
by changing flowers, that in succession write
their coloured names, their scent upon the air.

He lived by seasons and their need, on land,
she lived in sea, a subject of the moon,
he was time's child and vassal, born to die,
she was beyond, below, above; too soon
these differences like a stormy sky
promised them winter gales and torn sea-strand.

For land must hold the farmer to his trade
call back the lover to his beasts and byres
use all his skill and steal his time away;
and life warms hands beside the homely fires
that cook the food and greet the early day
and from these busy hours full years are made.

Hopeless and brief the autumn burned away,
cold sea-storms broke their refuge in the cove
and each one's vision of the other died
towards the withering torment of lost love.
Each to the other sad, accusing, cried
'Why will you leave me and not share my way?'

Hearts break, and parting fills the world with tears,
and yet, outliving the small span of joy,
the pattern of delight, if truly set,
has power that no future can destroy
and stands beyond the terrors of regret
to shed a blessing on succeeding years.

And so he found it; life simple, richly spent,
a prospering farm inherited in youth,
a village wife with ebony black hair,
a new wing to the farm-house, facing south –
such things the cold sea-creature could not share
though her lost radiance shone on his content.

Her story was his lifetime, spent in memory,
living while he remembered their shared days
then vanishing, changed back to foam and light,
restored to elements. But still their story stays
haunting this shore and told on winter nights,
where inland, inland you can hear the sea.

Here, in his lulling peace the landsman lies
who loved a mermaid once. Cut in his stone
blurred by moss, dimmed by a century's weather
you see her outline, carved and overgrown
beside his name, remembering them together.
Sleep, landsman, sleep between the sea and skies.

The Garden of Delights

After the cliffs, the desert and despair,
footsore, thirsty, desperate and cold
the traveller finds the shadow of a wood,
through weeping trees vistas of fear unfold.
He gropes from thought to thoughts not understood.
Although this ending has been mapped and told
he stumbles on still clutching at the air.

But when the darkness parts at last he sees
beyond the leafless trees lie a deep glade
and there perpetual spring in all its joys
buds, sings and dances through the light and shade.
No lurking terrors threaten or destroy,
the air is birdsong, flowers do not fade
though golden apples shimmer on the trees.

No pause, no change within though all without,
the moment passionately dreamed through years
lies at my feet, a path through summer grass;
how shall I see it through this mist of tears?
Here my search ends, no boundary left to pass,
and having come unscathed through fires and fears
why should I stand before my joy in doubt?

How can such weary arms as these embrace,
or faithful hands that tore their way through night
so scarred and bruised fold love against my breast,
or eyes that learned the shadows look on light,
or heart bewildered suddenly be at rest?
Having come so far to seek for this delight
I stand in darkness still and hide my face.

Let the last courage now inform my way
and ardent truth that showed the first steps clear
shine on the ending of this lifelong quest.
Let love and wisdom in my sight appear
as the first vision showed them, whole and blest.
Turn back, my weariness; turn back, my fear;
for single-hearted I accent the day.

Certainty

In this silence, peace enclosed,
in your arms, with heart at rest,
firelight, moonlight, midnight round us,
comforted, assuaged and blest,
quiet beyond all dreams of quiet
joy lies entranced on hand and breast.

For this plenty sheds its bounty,
touches grief now years away:
to the desperate tears of morning,
to that self, from now, I say
'all is found, and your enchanted
steps t'will lead you to this day.'

Far, and on what unknown landscape
like a lighthouse beam is cast
this moments' certainty and refuge
for the future as the past.
Between our hands and in their keeping
Love has found its peace at last.

Quiet, beyond all dreams of quiet
joy lies entranced on hand and breast.
Within this silence, peace enclosed,
comforted, assuaged and blest,
firelight, moonlight, midnight round us
past and future lie at rest.

The thing that hath been

it is that which shall be; and that which is done is that which shall be done: and there is no new thing under the sun.

Ecclesiastes 1, 9.

As inland shells tell of a sea withdrawn
that now lie dry and hollow in the sun
so is this temple a shadow of man's grace
whose years are over and whose time is done;
here was his spirit's shelter and resting place,
his towers were angels, his ramparts dark and dawn.

As inland shells lie empty to the day
where once some tiny creature had its hold
and shaped a curious spiral to its need,
so nave and transept stand deserted, cold,
their builder as forgotten as his creed:
the stones endure though man has gone away.

What wonder stands for truth among the blind
until their groping hands touch certainty?
What music builds its pinnacles in air
unheard among the deaf? What heresy
dares dream that timeless firmaments should wear
only such aspects as man's senses find?

When morning first divided dark from light
it taught man's eyes to see nothing alone
but all things rooted in their history,
wattles foreshadowing high vaulted stone,
and his hands learned their gradual mastery
as he pursued vision's wide winging flight.

Shaped by the fugitive spirit on its way,
cut into screen and boss and canopy,
the gods and angels of lost faith remain
the Powers and Virtues of a Hierarchy
sheltering man, who like a chieftain slain
lies by his consort in death's stone array.

Now that their words have vanished into air,
leaving no trace of what they might have told,
silence is earth and air and wind and wave
and sight is lost beneath an eyelid's fold.
Love lies by Man upon his six-foot grave,
pride at his head and at his foot despair.

Sleep, sleep in stone my warrior Mankind,
sleep Love with folded hands against your breast,
crouch servant Pride, and humble dog, Despair;
a thousand centuries are little rest
before this alabaster wakes to share
another coil the universe unwinds.

The preacher said that what has been shall be,
nothing is ever new under the sun:
late in our fading wisdom we have found
inanimate and animate are one.
Life's wandering spirit is never to be bound
but sojourns or sleeps within mortality.

Compose yourself my body to this rest;
yield to the lonely silence of the night
whose coming burns this vision on your eyes;
yield all your senses, all that was delight;
since you were born you knew that beauty dies.
Yield, for the darkness climbs about your breast.

But let the gesture of your stony hands
tell of your love, of honour and not fear.
And let this mask, stone image of your face
cry out for evermore that life was here;
from your stone limbs be born a later race.
Against the night your towering angel stands.

In my end is my beginning

I

Propped on a broken jamb, the garden door
opens on deserts. It opened here before
on branchy orchards, cool all summer through,
coloured and scented, drenched in light and dew.

The fire and power, fury of being alive
survive my spring, dried to the very bone,
and drive me to the wilderness that lies
beyond my ruins, waiting for me alone.

Alone is more than solitary now,
horizon to horizon footmark spanned,
where self learns self, walking companionless,
a single thread across striated sand:

it is the day that withers into age;
it is the sleepless night on which I lie
a hieroglyph, bare pattern of mankind,
under the changing star-map of the sky:

it is the sense that none was here before,
no kindred creature ever breathed this air
or left a trace of life as wayside alms
or token of known hope or known despair.

Stumbling and tattered flesh will you endure?
will you outlast the soul's eternity
to spin a maze with no deliverance
on empty earth below the empty sky?

I am the miraged desert and the restless sea,
the dumb beast, blind and quivering, drenched in fear
or burning in the hollow hand of day:
the whole of grief caged in a single tear.

Anguish of time rise up and flower in me,
wake springs from-rocks and summon back delight,
blessing and healing flow from a broken hand,
where the dumb remember words, the blind learn sight.

Life, in Love's image made, defaced and marred
never obliterate, still with honour tell
man's princeliness, affirm creation's truth
speaking in words made before Babel fell.

All landmarks lost: no sandstone Memnon left
singing to sunrise: and no cities' trace
lies humped in dust with all its glory down
to make a shadow in the wilds of space.

What voice can answer here but my own voice ?
What shadow fall but mine? What can be known
beyond my knowledge? But suddenly, face to face
Love stands before me here and is my own.

Whose hands cut out these features on the rock?
Whose vision knew these leaf-veined fans as wings ?
Who saw those eyes would hold the depths of space,
those hands the source whence living water springs ?

Who came before me all this desert way,
endured such night and then outlived such day
to tear divine assurance from the stone,
this first and last, this sum of all things known ?

II

I was an echo of a far-off sound,
a thorn of shadow cast along the ground
now gathered up to stature of a god.
My empty hands touched earth, therein to find
the source of rivers, their deep springs unbind:
wings spread about me, feather and filament
alert with life and power for ascent.

Manifest love, flame fallen to aspire,
burning to consume and not destroy,
infinite meaning, crown and crest of fire,
what words interpret and yet not alloy
the absolute vision, consummated joy?

Love has no shadow: one with living light,
daybreak unfurled upon the ebbing night
and exultation blazing through the sky,
I hold eternity within my hand;
a drop of water or a grain of sand,
what more was I
who am life's self, love's self to glorify?

III

The world's end lies where journeys were begun:
by quays with iron chains looped through the sea,
and rust-red hulks whose seafaring is done
and umber nets stretched drying in the sun.

The world's end lies in this familiar place;
first outward footmark is the last footstep home,
the thread is joined, woven to leave no trace
or knot this moment as a point in space:

Up the same lane to the same garden door
where all the early world of morning lies,
rain strung on sunlight through the grassy floor
and April branches flowering evermore.

Speak now my senses, in whose light I move
from radiance to radiance through the day
where heavy trees echo the clouds above;
keep your perpetual festival of love.

O apprehended self, so long unknown
beyond the tides of growth and withering,
to such a benediction you have grown
within the temporal ramparts of the bone.

Love is man's measure and his wisdom's end:
in joy's uncertainty and known despair,
he seeks no other state for heart or mind,
no peace beyond the glories they can find.

O child of substance and the elements,
charting your journey by this wandering star,
what can you make more than the thing you are?

Taking part in Spencer's Epithalamion as a Masque

His hymn to love held in one summer day
the innocence of joy and endless hope,
tranquil security of heart to heart,
long years of promise and felicity.
Bells singing in the towers
to measure out the hours
yet to be worn away,
till to stillness, through enchanted silence,
he in her beauty lost, she in his love,
they pass together to their solitude,
dreaming, beyond our sight,
lit by stars, blessed by the tender night.

I wear her garlands, where her way was love
mine lies in music, mirror to that fire
showing ghost beauty at its zenith still,
a midsummer outlasting centuries.
I give my heart for both,
my truth to be her troth,
flame in her flame I move
among the echoes and among the dancers.
Once incarnatus' woke the wondering flesh,
and still it sings the safety of all joy
while music brings them from eternity
to live our vision of their bridal day.

The Sleepness Night

'Pretender to the day lay down your arms:
native and heir to darkness find your home,
a primitive inheritance of night,
kingdom of terror; worlds before time was made
recall you to their shade.'

Safety usurped, behind whose walls I dwell,
where senses set their limit and their rule,
how shall I leave you, O my sleeping city
Merciless darkness summons me again;
'Lay down your arms.'
Resistance is in vain.

Along the boundary of its territory
ghosts on their humble business in the house
whisper and shuffle in the corridors:
penned in the measure of Time's hour-glass
their dead reflections pass.

All easy commerce with the light is done
Worn out and laid aside, its patterns fade,
alarms increase, grow forest-high and wild
to shade despair beside a lake of tears
and shelter preying fears.

There are no weapons for the batt!e here:
Horror's cold fingers lay shackles on the hands
and chain the feet, leaving no escape;
while memory with tentacles of pain
searches the secret brain.

I made this kingdom of my solitude.
With idle scrawl marked on a careless chart
I drew the outline of these seas of grief,
cast countless seeds of nightmare, carelessly,
that choke dear memory.

Behind the lonely windows of the dark
in deserts bordering chaos, beyond Time,
ruler and captive, abandoned to defeat,
I wait to seize upon the earliest light
to build my walls of sight.

The Beginning

Eve woke in Eden. Bright creation lay
perfect around her, home for every sense,
eloquent in perception of the day:
she, as all living creatures sharing its innocence,
had no memory of disseverance
till Adam woke: beyond that radiance
of recognition, morning's magnificence,
she saw divergence of their mortal way.

Fable of one made two, division known
only when healing seals the wound again
as spirit cries to spirit, bone to bone,
showing their fiery evidence of pain
to prove each other self each other's own.
The tokens match and yet they match in vain.

Silence and Music

(1959)

Stonehenge

By whose desire at what command
do stones stand circle on the plain
strangers that dominate the land
worn by wind and marred by rain
though quarried once by human hand?

Gate for the summer sun to enter,
grove where moon's darkest shadows fall
palisading edge and centre
when snow and silence cover all
desolate at night in winter.

Sand quivers to a bow-drawn note
and trumpets-raze a city wall,
bird song, one small distended throat
is summer's voice while centuries fall
like grass swathes at a mower's foot.

The power of music hung each star
circling in the firmament:
a memory of that strength could dare
lead stones across a continent
beguiled by an immortal air.

Set free from prisoning rocks they came
like pilgrims to a holy place,
joyful in some god's power and name
made animate by strength and grace
swift and glorious, crowned with flame.

Some singing priest with king and slave
led them on that triumphant march
where stone walked lightly on the wave
and followed hill and forest path
to stand here in a hallowed grove.

So far in time from parent hill,
and so far inland from the sea,
the utmost reach of might and skill
set them as a sanctuary
where sun fulfils their ritual.

Not one remembers, no winds sing
one word of that lost music now,
or they would break their holy ring
and in a ghost procession go
after its echo following.

Joshua Trees in the Desert

This is no forest: no word for wood or grove,
all that we know as tree is here denied,
none of our words can fit, nor the winds move
this race of beings half whose life has died.

Somewhere, shallow under desert dust
they may have roots, gnarled and twisting trails
that grope for damp, water for which they lust
comes to them rarely, furiously, then fails.

So they stand still with arms and hands upraised
attitudes frantic of anguish and despair,
two arms or six, the gestures are all phrased
and almost scream the bitter thirst they share.

Some have a broken neck and hanging head,
some bow themselves abandoned, to entreat,
some lie sprawled and black, humanly dead,
and all of them are withered by the heat.

If there was one, but one, that could be seen
still standing proudly or with dancing grace,
one who wore plume or frond of green
then there would be a hope for the whole race:

Hope for a spring; but spring does not come here,
these, born from prehistoric jungle seed
have waited generations in their fear,
have thirsted centuries in famished greed.

Fire could make men look like this nightmare host,
their bodies' language, mime of agony,
is likeness of mankind with all joy lost
yet life enough to suffer and not die.

Corneal Graft

At death I gave away my eyes,
translated by a surgeon's knife,
light for eyeballs dark since birth;
is it my sight revisits earth,
taking another span of life
until my heir, successor, dies?

A separate film to grow afresh,
insensate iris all I gave;
yet, if my living love should chance
to see them in a stranger's glance
should I not rise from past and grave
usurp that stranger's life and flesh?

My eye would hold and lock his sight
my bearer dumb before him stand
as grafted nerves spoke to his heart;
using live roots, my flowers would start,
spring up and cover all the land
with petals bred from weeping night.

Will one who wears my eyes in sleep
see my dreams, or do they fade?
My legacy, my jewels, hold
no trace of silver clasp or gold
no chain or locket time once made
sapphire and emerald light to keep.

I died and gave my eyes away;
I needed none, for my dark night
is lighted by another fire;
a torchbearer that will not tire
my heart burns in celestial light,
my eyes are surety for this day.

All Souls' Day

This is the day for ghosts: from dawn they crowd
and through our homes their human memories tread;
the present is busy in time and unaware
of all that silver thronging in the air,
deaf to the words still trembling to be said,
words that must perish, take no shape aloud.

They wait for us to summon, ours the choice
to heal, complete and make peace with the shade
longed for in early, unfamiliar grief:
they seek us now for quittance or relief,
they come to us, while heedless or afraid
we will not call them to us and rejoice.

Absence was presence felt when grief was fresh,
now we have power to live without our dead
and being safe refuse to give release,
unloose their fetters with a word of peace
withheld sometime by fireside, table, bed,
nor dream that spirits wear the scars of flesh.

A last leaf falls down past the moon's face,
the rags of memory flutter in the wind
old, dusty banners in the architrave:
awake in gardens, the cocks of morning crow,
earth gathers back her ghosts. Each living mind
leaps towards morning's light and well-known place.

And this is failure and victory in one.
We have held silence, not a voice has spoken
across the chasm, having no love to spare.
Ghosts, being jealous of our mortal air,
we built that paradise where you have woken
under another moon, another sun.

Spells laid in winter

She

The window lies like ice between two nights,
the indoor night of echoes in the heart,
the outdoor night of moonless stillness, cold,
cold grass, cold silence; and all fold
the whole world in this summary of sights
that lie beyond glass boundaries apart.

I stand indoors and burn and shake and burn,
the unconsumed, the tree caught in a flame
whose winter stems, taught by this sudden heat,
force out the buds, so snow and petals meet
in white and white before the flowers turn
to fruitless ashes, fall and leave no name.

I stand indoors with fingers on the pane
drawing the cold night inwards through my eyes
till all the landscape freezes round a thought;
a net, a snare, a cage of hours has caught
my fiery frenzy that blazes up and dies
while moonrise radiance and the frost remain.

Cold is a spell of peace, a night of rest
breaking the torment of the burning mind:
this is the longed-for winter of the earth,
barrenness more absolute than birth,
an age of ice she lays against her breast
that growth and movement into stillness bind.

Rest is this lapse of pain: it will endure
as short a time as moonlight, it will wane,
be lost for ever. On a snowy bridge I stand
above a chasm: now at my command
shut in a zircon, a pale jewel's flaw
a wall of ice around a depth of pain.

See, from this hour of peace I will cry out
summon those messengers that strength can call.
One hand is fire, the other ice, they lie
upon the window pane, against the sky,
my power grasps the poles, untouched by doubt
I could command the stars and make them fall.

"All the winds that rise and blow
across the earth, across the sea,
winds that men have named and know,
and the faintest stirring breeze
on winter nights when rivers freeze,
give me ease.

By the flames upon the hearth,
by the fires that follow war,
by the blazing comet's path
his steps I draw,
to me, I draw.

Water of life where I would drink
waters of death where all must go
unquiet seas the edge and brink
of earth and parting ebb and flow,
teach and show.

Let every air
Let every place
Let fire and water
my image wear.
In every thought
and dream and sound
in word and echo
let me be found."

He

"I see with every beast's uncoloured sight
men have gone home, men live inside the days
then sleep in shuttered houses till the dawn.
Into this other world my life is drawn
this land of monochrome, of dark and silver greys,
shadows and colourless substances of night.

Each tree has learned a different song to sing
its song-bird, daytime voices are asleep
now they cry out from root and branch and sap,
rock plumes of mistletoe or let the ivy wrap
their scars of branches lost for which they weep,
or stretch twigs to the wind like a wide open wing.

In the long conjuration of the wind
there's a lost language: though the words are gone
familiar phrases cry and call the heart
back to the source of dreams where memories start
and stir the ancient dust, fable and stone,
that hide the springs of time in every mind.

This is a forest where a century sleeps
marking no change on dreaming breast and brow
of the enchanted one who waits for love.
I am led here, each thicket is a grove
to let me pass where briar and nightshade grow;
but darkness shivers and her window weeps."

Echo

The charred tree fell on ash and snow,
black windows show no light within,
but bear the distant moon's device
a sable shield where flowers of ice
climb on the glass and fronds begin
to weave a forest where none may go.

Menelaus on the Beach at Pharos

You will come home, not to the home you knew
that your thought remembers, going from rose to rose
along the terraces and staying to gaze
at the vines and iris beside the lake
in the morning haze.

Forgetting the place you are in where the cold sea winds go
crying like gulls on the beach where horned sea poppies grow.

Homesick wanderer, you will come home
to a home more ancient, waiting your return:
sea frets the steps that lie green under waves
and swallows nest below lintel and eaves:
there lamps are kindled for you, they will burn
till you come, however late you come,
till the west wind's sheltering wing
folds round your sail and brings you to land.

Stretch out your hand,
murmuring lapping sea and the lamps and the welcome wait
to draw you home to rest.
You shall come home and love shall fold you in joy
and lay your heart on her breast.

The Youngest Son

Man came last: his elders, winged and armoured
fought for pasture, each against the others,
for water-holes or caves, or went away
till all the world was peopled with their play.
Then man rose up and tamed or killed his brothers

till no vast dragons lived fiercely in the forests
no more huge flight darkened the open sky,
only the working beasts, forced to his will,
or small, wild targets for the hunter's skill
were left to fringe his world and bear his mastery.

So man grew older, rich, in silk pavilions
played with flowering times and wreathed his lance
with banners for his formal wars, and found
death's face in an hour-glass was no bound
to the proud human spirit in its dance.

In sweeping dirge and splendid requiem
he called on light's celestial counterpart
to be his soul's new universe in death,
stretched his hand beyond life's little breath
and made a heaven and hell out of his heart.

Beauty his consort, pride his native state
power his object, he conquered land and sea,
tamed the elements to suit his need,
lighted the darkness, transplanted season, seed,
grew in magnificence and monarchy.

Then, grown beyond all reason, deep out of earth
he dug remembered dragons' iron bones,
fledged them with armoured flesh, mechanic growth,
rebuilding all the monsters of his youth
that once he killed with arrows and with stones.

So man has come the long way home to fear,
the little, naked, cleverer-than-the-rest
has made himself the dragon that he slew,
imagination shows him nothing new
gathering annihilation to his breast.

Jacob and the Angels

When I was young the angels came as light
descending to my sleep,
a dream for sense to keep,
an arrogant vision illuminating night.

There in the desert world of dust and stone
no pillow for my rest,
my solitude was blest,
my journey and my halting place were known.

Never again has firecrest, flame-winged truth
descended from the sky
to seek me where I lie
as then the angels filled the dream of youth.

In middle years the angels came as fear,
walking the roads I know,
bent heads, absorbed and slow,
I heard them speak because they passed so near:

but not for me those shining words were said,
star speaks to star in light,
rays tossed from flight to flight
seen by man's eyes but uninterpreted.

When I was old, one angel came alone,
dark to my mortal eyes
he came in night's disguise;
we touched to wrestle until one was thrown.

Hip flanged on hip and palm to palm we grew
closed in our emnity
while all night's stars streamed by;
lost in each other no separate world we knew.

My failing limbs withered against his pride
and thence drew strength again
to master all the pain
that numbed my hands and crawled along my side.

When daybreak cocks crowed the horizon round
morning was my tower,
in light I rose, in power,
and from my angel's heart blessing and love unbound.

One shadow lay on dew beneath our feet,
one look between our eyes,
voices, one voice that cries
rejoicing in both victory and defeat.

All that divided us had made us one.
I was the angel, he was I,
and earth held all winged sky
clasped in the bounty of the morning sun.

The Girl in the Wood

Rain fell: I stood at the verge of green woods,
leaving petticoats under a cherry tree,
tumble of emerald and cambric under branches,
naked, entreating spring to speak to me,

ankle deep in violets by a step,
the house has gone, its floor a primrose bed,
no roof but growing branches, no wall or window,
but a quince, unpruned and unhindered spread.

'Threshold of man where the forest enters,
gate of return, I come with empty hands,
with rain on my hair as the rain adorning your leaves,
a sister to Daphne and Syrinx stands,

younger than oak, sooner to die than beech,
sharing spring with hawthorn, cherry and rose,
suppliant I come to you trees, to question your wisdom
where in the woods the tree of knowledge grows.'

Tranced in a silence of rain and doves I stood,
ardent to learn the words and truth of spring.
The rain ended and the sun glowed torwards sunset
brushed leaf and hand and every feathered wing.

Then rustling steps stirring old, fallen leaves,
there came a red fox brushing past my knee,
unafraid and kin: clear language of his golden eye
reflected all that I had wished to be.

In a Studio

(Self Portraits)

See, I was this girl, quiet, translucent, less
or was I more, being rich in future then?
painting a face upon a summer field,
painting a muslin dress,
a century of years ago, or ten,
a wish unfolding and a thought concealed.

If I used words I'd name that face 'disguise',
the skill I used suggests experience,
shaped hair and cheek and mouth and all I see
to lead towards the eyes
and there I look. That was, but is not, me
gazing on flowers with subtle innocence.

Now I confront another kind of grace
and try to capture beauty's last touch of pride,
shimmer of movement before the darkening rain
falls on this tine and place:
and shall I find, ten gears having passed again,
another thought than this I do not hide?

Again I paint the face I see. I give
ancestral features human, passionate sense,
truth and proportion, form, colour and light.
Rapt in power I live;
my hand moves with my thought, sure and intense;
from the canvas an unknown face appears.

Martha

If I am dumb, my hands speak to the earth;
the rain, the soil, the sun bring flowers forth
but I have set the vines and pruned the roses,
at my command hedge beyond hedge encloses
the needed herbs and all the seasons' plenty.

Instinct, not thought, fosters my care that glows
on furniture and floors, the light that flows
out into night comes from lamps I keep.
I cherish order from waking until sleep;
no life can thrive without this simple bounty.

If I am loveless, a body moving to age,
yoked in service, I have a living wage
giving continuance of fire and bread:
no hearth remembers, and the hungry, fed,
do not recall the sowing, the green corn.

My hands receive the newborn and the dead
I am their welcome. I make the marriage bed,
I lay the coins on the earth-closed eyes.
I am life's minister, my toil is to be wise;
my heart is proud, my humble hands are worn.

The Hermit

(Ramon Lull)

Love turned from love: all that had been one face,
a dazzling body and lace-shadowed hair,
has driven my heart to seek another grace:
the impress of a bird's flight on the air
is not more lost than she death walks beside:
her path is set, my way is still world-wide.
O discipline of grief,
I am her exile, I her unbelief.

Love turned to love; and I must learn 'no more'
can be as rich in promise as denial.
Eyes fringed with dream look for a waking shore
unmeasured by a clock of hours, sun's dial.
The voice of solitude
is a harsh speaker of beatitude.

Earth bears all change, accepts famine or flood,
but earth has time that will outlive a heart:
grief parches man as autumn bares a wood,
and if the one who hopes, and hope, must part
accent the fallen tree,
its fruit is gathered for eternity.

I left the shaded city for bare rock.
The mountain gives me all the coasts of night,
I stand on clouds, the constellations flock
my mountain side, I pasture in their light
till sunrise fills my hands
and wakes the incense of these barren lands.

Love turned to love: the discipline of pain
has taught my body to rejoice alone:
my spirit wakes, tears are a fertile rain
to quicken flowers from the unyielding stone.
O love, be love set free
not a caged, desperate life to die with me.

The Beauchamp Tomb at Worcester Cathedral

Make me an effigy, and let it wear
my living, sleeping face. Fold my hands in prayer
and shape stone pearls to bind and net my hair;
my stateliest dress spread out to fold and flare
brocaded summer to the chantry air;
all that adorns my life shall, echoed, share
the long endurance of my beauty there.
And when my husband comes to claim his bed
in his stone likeness, I will have it said
he seeks a woman in whose sleep still shows
his other self, who was his noonday rose.
And let my head lie pillowed evermore
on a swan's wing in sable heraldry
night-feathered singer of a single song
floating on time where our drowned shadows lie.
Let my love's head rest on another wing,
my swan shall stay for his by this aisled shore
for side by side our effigies belong.
At this rejoining all the bells shall sing.
Memorial beauty, alabaster sleep
in ceremony we meet with death to keep
our marriage vows, and here we shall arise
clothed for the courts of heaven and for each other's eyes.

'The word of lyf show unto us'

Miles Coverdale

The winter breathes its garlands on the glass
and indoors, fire tamed to its cage, the hearth
comforts the watcher who is charmed to stillness
while light flakes hide and cover grass and path
and shed a dream of blossom on the trees,
white where the may was red, the lilac dark,
making a winter night an arctic day
hiding all boundaries, blotting each footstep's mark.

The world we know is hidden under snow;
another shines upon us; eyes now learn
strange landmarks where familiar sight is stayed,
two visions of one place; each will return
in sequence to renew the seasons' circling,
as tall midsummer grass and starlit frost
seem chance and change that lightly come and go,
winter in summer, summer in winter lost.

There was a harvest goddess I have seen
belonging to the world, summer and day,
beauty serene and stately, made by man;
two thousand years under the sea she lay,
her noon, her vines, acres of barley fields
all drowned and waste, a desert of sea sand,
where seaweed fronds floated across her eyes
and hollow shells lay broken in her hand.

Water had claimed her as it claimed the town,
breaking on sleep one winter night, and she,
calm watcher over plenty, could not stay
the leaning waves nor still the shouting sea
that threw down walls and levelled all the towers,
drowned a wide plain to make another bay
where later fishermen put out to sea
and drew her up in nets and back to day.

The bronze remains; two thousand years of sea
have left unchanged the knotted hair, calm eyes
that smiled on morning in forgotten fields:
one hand upon a drooping sheaf still lies
holding their harvest, the other, lifted arm,
is raised in blessing, giving with open hand
protection to all young and growing things,
vinyards and flowers of a generous land.

When nets drew her from the sea's possession
she seemed to be love rising once again,
the unknown face that all men recognise,
search for in mortal faces and pursue in vain,
grasp, lose or find in dreams under the moon:
love in fulfilment and mystery were there.
They brought her home with garlands to the town
roses and coral crowning her sea-wet hair.

She was two thousand years under the sea,
she was a statue of man's hope of joy,
of harvest bounty and of sheltering love:
a beauty that sea-fret could not destroy,
for time is nothing to man's persisting dream,
so many harvests, so many falling snows,
births, deaths and loves, perfections made and lost
under the changeless flowering of the rose.

The poet waits through centuries for an hour
when he shall both possess and bear the earth,
triumphant draw his thought up from the deep
of chaos apprehended before birth.
The moment comes and he commands the sun,
new rivers spring between his mighty hands,
his palm and instep wear the stigmata
and he alone in naked glory stands.

How shall this vigil be endured by man
whose winter draws so quickly on to night?
What must he dare to stand in pride and power
holding the world within his eagle sight?
It is no triumph, no gay garlanding,
this is a hunt, a chase that must be run,
all forms life takes are forms he too must learn,
drown in the sea, wither in desert sun.

The voices give their warning through the night,
between the snowflakes fall I hear them cry:
'Do not presume to claim the tongues of fire,
the word of life is not for those who die,
it is ringed round by all the powers of air,
hidden by earth and guarded by the sea;
you will fall prey to talon, fang and claw
if you adventure after mastery.'

Between the snow's quiet fall and silence lies
a passage wide enough for one to dare;
open the window and let in the cold
and I'll go out into the starry air;
no certainty can name this journey's end,
I must go barefoot, without human light,
a postulant possessing only need,
to find the way that is both search and flight.

My search is known, and so the hunt is up.
I who pursue am quarry, hoped-for prey,
abandoning the articulate pain of man
for pelt, fin, feathers; I cannot hide or stay,
the hunters hold the scent and follow fast,
hot as hound's breath closing on the hare,
parting her fur against her shrinking flank,
otter after fish, hawk stooping from the air.

'Earth takes me not, I am not her beast.
Water rejects me, I am not her own.
Sky drives me down again and back to earth.
Change as I will, still my intent is known;
even the barndoor fowl, the scratching hen
clucking in dust, filling her crop with grain
finds the anonymous seed; and lowly death attained
I wait as nothing to be born again.'

Go further still, beyond this baneful chase,
stripped of time, of sense and memory
nameless, cold, even wholly without self,
barely a shadow by the archaic sea
on whose black waves darkness broods unbroken;
this is the watch and vigil I must stay,
a trance that holds before transfiguration,
the sleepless prelude to the break of day.

Raise me from here, this brink where nothing is,
stretch out creation's hand that I may rise,
clothe me with flesh again and let me go,
breathe in my nostrils and unbind my eyes.
Far sought magnificence, on breast and tongue
the fire burns: eyes see and ears can hear
the singing stars, language of lion and tree,
all glory and all sorrow I must bear.

All lost lies somewhere, waiting to be found,
the golden apples scattered on the grass
under the tree still to be harvested.
Even two thousand years of vigil pass,
the red rose flowers, twining with the white
to crown a goddess risen from the sea,
a gift for lovers who slept long apart
and meet on thresholds of eternity.

But I am mortal still, my flesh is made
of earth's known summers and the frozen night:
there are still years to claim and words to speak;
the glowing cherubim in seagull flight
unfold their wings to bound the orchard's green.
I may not stay, for where the earth fires burn
only my frost rimmed footsteps mark the snow;
the open window waits for my return.

The Dictated Theme

I

All that was home lies under those arched lids,
no quiver stirs their hemispheres of night:
nothing has changed, but the beating heart is stilled,
and no blood pulses hearing now, or sight.

All that was home is left by those cool hands,
relinquishing the morning and the day,
folding their deep tranquillity and peace,
with all remembered years, stilly away.

All that was love remains and will not go,
until the lover meets him in some night
like this one, with its early waking birds
and all forgotten flowers again, in sight.

All that was joy remains, but is unseen
beyond this moment's tears, and they are less
than sighs indrawn on the marvellous day
that wakes in distance and will come to bless.

All that was whole is like a broken ring,
one half is his, and one half still is mine,
and time will join them somewhere and remake
an image even the shadow knew divine.

II

Being widowed is the empty arms at night,
the single plate, the room where no one comes,
the memory that cannot meet a smile,
and all the simple pattern of our homes.

Being faithful is the richness of the days,
the tenderness of nights, the hopes and fears
gathered and cancelled in each other's eyes,
the deep serenity of growing years.

Being yours is to shine still, for you unseen,
to wake and turn to where your sleep was blessed,
the last goodnight, the waking morning hour,
your hand contented on my heart at rest.

III

I give you back to the free elements,
I will not hate the flame's deliverance,
the phoenix burns, and rises plumed and free.

You gave your body with the marriage ring,
you left it in my arms, and this I bring
to give you quittance of mortality.

No more in time will hand's companionship
comfort and hold me, no more lip to lip
communicate abundance or desire.

And yet the morning like a wedding day
is golden plenty, and we go away
attended by a radiance to the fire.

Be free from any tie that holds and stays,
be free to go, but all my good, my days,
are lit from your bright being and will shine.

The heart is sure and claims no other sign.

IV

In dreams and reassurances I live,
in hours and days I cannot move alone,
I go to love by stony, secret ways,
the briars fall back as if my way was known.

However far the distance to the end
I know the home and haven of my heart;
however long the spring and summer seem
that bring no new-sown harvest to my part,

I know the task will bear allotted fruit.
I know the weight my hands hold till they break,
I know the darkness as I know the light,
and all the trials my self must undertake.

No doubt unless the gates of hell are closed
and barred against my coming to their door,
and even then my way must penetrate
and stumble certain through each corridor.

Through caves where each direction offers ways
failure and promise, till I find the right,
and in the heart of death's corruption lies
disguised, despised, what must arise to light.

Follow me, follow: I can penetrate,
touch with the hand of love, and even name
disintegrate, ignoble enmity
that breaks the body with dissolution's shame.

What once was man, and loved in tender arms,
what once was joy, see, I can clothe anew
in names of love, and so recall to form,
and broken feet heal with my tears of dew:

compel the housings to be whole and brave,
compel the little to reclaim the great.
Come from this ash, this dust, to stand again
apparelled in man's beauty and man's state.

O counterpart, O love, this woman's work
is three part harmony, to be your love,
to be the full maturity of mind,
the ear of wheat, the white and visiting dove:

and last, to be the aged ministration
to close the eyes and fold the hands at rest,
the folded silence and the sculptural sheet
that lie against the stillness of your breast.

All these are done, and in another sense
I bear your body back again to give
you who are me, I who am you, to prove
our being whole, and the whole being live.

So shall the singing birds repeat the spring,
so shall the corn stand in its golden state,
so shall the waters nourish our return,
and time undo its long unopened gate.

V

Simple to speak, and now no words are needed,
thought frames a pattern more intense.
Simple to love, the heart beats on unchanged,
touch is the widowed sense.

Simple to lack, and easy to forget
the man of meaning in this new immense,
unwalled by time or hope of homecoming.
Touch is the widowed sense.

Simple to hope and in hope estrange
anguish, the true companion and defence
against the tide of day's inconsequence.
Touch is the widowed sense.

VI

If time had given us another hour,
and offered grace to part, time for farewell,
what could words have shaped from heart to heart,
what more to say that past years did not tell?
Nothing, I think, but that your head should lie
another hour pillowed on my arm,
nothing of me, all yours, you did not know
and nothing I could ask as life-long charm
to hold against the powers that divide
hand from hand, lip from lip separate,
no hour say more than all our lives had said,
so nothing stayed death's swift, commanding state.

VII

Are you a presence or a dream, I question:
are you yourself, invisible at my side?
Or have you stayed in my heart and thought so long
the impression, like a hare's form on the hillside
is deeply marked, so grasses will never grow
but bent to hold your shadow, curved and low?

Are you beside my sleep when I'm not there
but lost in night, lost beyond waking's sense?
Are you still the breath that is life in my living,
or is it memory, insistent and intense
I learned so long and now repeat again,
the echo music returning in refrain?

Are you? I ask, and who but I can tell?
I claim nothing, and do not ask you 'stay'.
Why here, when you in some far other state
are freed from dimension, as from night and day
unless you suffer too, suffer because no more
touch, sight or love are what they were before.

VIII

Look back and see, the past led to one place;
look now and see, nothing is clear or plain,
the mirage is the memory of one face,
all that has been cannot be again.

If there were tears before, why not more tears?
If there was solitude, it is not strange,
if there was hope, accept none for new years,
as there is death, I have acknowledged change.

Where there were two, one is to mourn or sing,
fire only burns till all's consumed to dust,
time is not long for elegies to bring
peace to unshared longings as it must.

Love and death are the pure themes of living,
destructable and sorrowful solitude,
the double being, locked hemispheres, unmoving
through desolation or beatitude.

IX

No longer bearing the weight and burden of time
you change, though change I cannot see,
yet by my side I sense the rising sap,
the breath of life, all truth's authority;
youth, with life's wisdom to its beauty given
perfected and made whole in this entirety.

I am the captive, I the one in chains
held by a sensual grief of time and place,
captive to memory that can with tears assail,
a travelled road that love can still retrace
to happiness and hope and long content,
not valid now, but shadows marked on space.

I know your freedom, it shall grow in me,
I know your love and mine shall match its light;
our pattern be the great birds that I saw
sweeping the sky in solitary flight,
flying for each other's far companionship
circling and meeting on the rim of sight.

Below, the earth is darkening to sleep,
the birds are burning in the upper sky,
pinioned in a morning sphere of light,
in intersecting arcs they poise and fly.
Wingless we are, but they, our heralds, keep
our meaning and our whole necessity.

Lead me for ever, as for ever past,
we came from far to be each other's own:
you go, and I still stay a summoning.
Though to the world's end each must come alone
welcome cannot be less than parting seems
nor we be separate whom love knows as one.

Silence and Music

Silence, come first: I see a sleeping swan,
wings closed and drifting where the water leads,
a winter moon, a calm where wisdom dreams,
a hand outstretched to gather hollow reeds.

The four winds in their litanies can tell
all of earth's stories as they weep and cry;
the sea names all the treasures of her tides,
and birds rejoice between the earth and sky:

voices of grief and from the heart of joy,
so near to comprehension do we stand
that wind and sea and all of winged delight
lie in the octaves of man's voice and hand

and music wakes from silence as from sleep.

Aspects

(1984)

They drink words

They drink words, lies flow on and on;
a river running in a filthy spate
quenches no thirst; corruption but infects
and poison's always recognized too late.

They eat words; a meal of rumour feeds
an appetite and crams a greedy mouth
with detritus and mould and sour decay,
they spoon them up, thinking they feed on truth.

They smell at words and like the carrion best;
they touch them too, paw with a curious hand
the blunted surface and the scurfing rust
littered through time and waste across the land.

Who would see words? Where shadow mars the form,
cut back the overgrowth to find again
the image man created, his first speech,
his cry of 'morning!' or his prayer, 'rain'.

Who would have words must marry silence first,
take thirst as discipline, hunger for food,
smell air, touch darkness, reclaim every need
before he speaks and speech is understood.

Man without Myth

He did not know his father was a tree
nor that his mother was a river's child,
that the sea rocked his cradle long ago
or that the birds came crowding from the wild
to tell him stories of their hierarchy
and teach him all the things a man should know.

He did not know his dog had ranged with stars
nor that his horse had wings he could not see,
his cat been known in temples of the sun.
All doors stand open to infinity.
He only saw a window dark with bars
and many little matters to be done.

He never saw his wife was made from flowers,
ephemeral beauty and enduring roots,
a forest murmur and a summer scent,
he only cared for the thirst-quenching fruits
and cursed her withering and autumn hours
and did not follow winter ways she went.

Nor did he know history as a road
on which he too made footprints every day.
He never used his head or heart or hand;
when comets blazed he looked the other way.
Small jealousy was something of a goad
but more than that he could not understand.

He never knew and never cared to know
more than bare necessity could show.
Once man and wonder walked life side by side:
he lost his kingdom when his magic died.

Jungles, whose growth is sudden in our sight

Jungles, whose growth is sudden in our sight,
who know that centuries must build an oak,
take only weeks to make their tenting dense
over man's empty roofs, to close and cloak
roadways and gateways. So impermanence
is demonstrated as the tendrils choke
a hovel or some old magnificence,
as silence fills the courtyards where men spoke.

If you, a wanderer, chance upon a stone
cut with a lettered language or a face
it's clue enough for knowledge to retrace
a city's plan, however overgrown.
So a name scribbled on a diary's page
brings back all youth to break the heart of age.

The Old Women

The game is long and sad each day,
the players do not know they play
sitting at gossip or at tea:
no cards, no counters, but they speak
names that are their conjuration
of once familiar hand or cheek.
They summon ghosts to stand beside
their white-lace memory of a bride,
shadow or an apparition.

All that is past has gained a gloss,
a patina that years and loss
have laid upon each history.
They do not cut or draw or toss
but bid their long soliloquies,
making new dreams of all that was.
All name perfection, none confess
to jealousy or fear or stress:
each Eve recalls her Paradise.

Each private glass reflects despair
but each curls up her pale, thin hair,
masters the change to 'I' from 'we'.
Courage the daily dress they wear
to hide their naked desolation,
descending slowly, stair by stair,
to play the long, exhausting game;
their counters are each dead man's name,
who have none, have no consolation.

The Silver Hound

Prologue

Memory is my silver hound
stalking days that time has hidden,
searching for a past that's lost
in shadows grown as thick as grass.
Give him courage, let him pass
find the secret and forbidden,
open graves and free each ghost.
Let my seven selves be found,
quarry for my silver hound.

Lullaby

I was a cradled child
who woke to see the stars.
I thought that I could touch the sky
beyond the window bars.

I heard the song of rain,
I laughed with morning light,
I smelled the budding leaves of spring,
and knew that sleep was night.

The bough was rocked; by wind,
the tree-top cradle fell.
I knew the cold of sudden fear
but had no words to tell.

The Schoolboy

When learning came,
tall as a giant, talking of centuries,
showing me measure, weight and volume,
teaching me dimension,
bringing me languages,
laying before me all of man's achievement,
I was amazed by all these opened doors,
enchanted by the music and the stories.
But, being young, I often turned away,
calling my friends to come with me to play.

The Soldier

Look in the mirror, soldier, soldier,
What do you see?
My share of pride, of courage, of duty
and victory.

Look at the prisoners, soldier, soldier,
What do you see?
My own reflection, my wounds, my hunger,
my enemy.

Look at the shrouded, soldier, soldier,
What do you see?
My shadow, my brother, my youth, my loss,
all history.

The Lover

My love has no measure,
but the words of other lovers.
Yet my hope is boundless, garlanded and certain.
I give my promise, I give my truth,
I commit my years to you with joy.
I ask nothing – I ask everything.
Do you understand this, Beauty,
as I speak to you in the words of other lovers?

The Statesman

I have served, so now I may command,
I have listened, now is the time to speak,
I have endured, now I offer justice.
Rich, let me remember poverty.
Fortunate, let me become wise.
Steel should not forget the pain of fire
to which it owes its strength.

The Old Man

I am my own ghost now,
dreams are my company.
Saplings I set are forest trees.
Love is an echo, home is a shadow.
I sit with a rug across my knees
while small birds feed on my window ledge.

Epitaph

What was your quarry, silver hound?
The dead man's name means little here.
What did you find, ranging through time,
his joy? his power? his youth, his fear?
Did seven selves make one man whole?

The Learning Heart

Words in their daily use grow thin and dim,
the smallest, not the utmost of their reach
– like easy shoes on a familiar road –
used without thought to answer thoughtless speech,
until a meaning burns into a life,
gives grief its weight, before, a thing unknown,
or joy, all radiance, shines as it is named
because its meaning is at last one's own.

Then, as inheritors, we see the gold,
sharp impress of an image as when new,
not blurred or dulled by all time's pastime-talk
but clear as the idea from which it grew.
So never after, on a printed page
or on a stranger's lips, will word be sound
without experience testing it again
against the essence recognized and found.

Old Letters, old Poems

Three ageing poets loved me when I was young,
they gave me verses, they gave me stories,
they praised my work, they said I was beautiful.
They spoke with knowledge of the craft they knew,
they laid their hopes on me as if they were garlands
and each one said 'If I was young again,
if I was young again I'd be your lover.'
I kissed them lightly, taking all this for kindness,
seeing myself as an echo of their lost hopes,
I took their last loves, their last poems,
being in love myself I thought of them as friends.
But now, being old as they were then, I know
they were in love as desperately as I
and all those poems were true.

'Ainsi le bon temps regrettons . . .'

No, I will not tell you with whom I danced,
nor of the music we knew;
we stepped through the window and danced on the terrace
onto the grass and danced by the water,
the music followed us.
But long ago the grass was scythed
and with it our shadows
that danced till morning.

I will not tell you what the poets said.
I tore up their letters when they died:
no one keeps laurel leaves for long –
they get too dusty.

Nor can I tell you of love
that was my landscape,
you would translate it and see another place.

I can only say I danced,
I kept letters and re-read them,
I was loved, I loved.
You can only think it strange
seeing me now.

Autobiography

I called them eagles, so they were all eagles
floating above a gulf of olive trees,
Parnassus skies and springs and prophecies
with falling stars and dancers in the night.

I thought of islands, so there were three islands,
each one in morning seas superb and calm,
a sycamore, a carob and a palm
against the firefly clustered Pleiades.

I knew it truth, so it became all truth,
my measure stood because I knew no other:
my only truth is that we stand together
even surrounded or when separate.

I name it solitude, so it is solitude
because no other truth can touch the years
that lie like islands till the sun appears
to shape their shores or show their boundaries.

I called it love, a name that has no proof,
so it was love, created and arising,
a bird of fire, feather from flame devising
in light that burns on all the world I know.

The Field of the Cloth of Gold

Night was pavilion for our meeting,
our ceremonial, witnessed by the stars,
acknowledging each other's lives as kingdoms.
We made no treaty, only brought our gifts.
With boundaries still unchanged, as they were mapped
before we came as princes to our pleasure,
we razed the walls that once marked our division
and planted corn and vines in celebration.

Latin between Lovers

In stately, formal language you express
timeless tenderness.
You call on older words than those we used
before our thoughts, like our locked hands, were fused.
You summoned history to witness and to bless
all we can give, all we may not possess.

Thaisa and Pericles

Solitude was remembering and forgetting
seas beat through silences and dedication
while years, like waves, drowned her desolation
deeper than she had thought a hope could drown
under each disciplined and ordered day
till she was calm and cold and unregretting.
Joy was a country that she had once known
and love a city centuries away.

When time's long mercy brought him to the land
where she had lived, and learned to live alone,
they reached across the separately known
and in the orbit of each other's sight
found resurrection neither had believed.
Their recognition, proved by lip and hand,
relived their morning in their evening light
in the astonishment of joy achieved.

This is the passionate ending to the play,
the sea-ringed story of a king and queen,
a death supposed, with all that death must mean
endured, but cancelled as they meet at last.
Will they now see each other as they are
or only as they were that storm-drowned day?
Will joy reclaimed be equal to joy past
or will lost grief be their most vivid star?

Words newly paired

When words are newly paired
their own becoming astonishes, enlightens.

Immediate present, in painted exploration,
endures, interprets and transfigures time.

Usual speech, unnoticed landscape, wear their strangeness
then blur again.

Familiar disregard comes easily.
Remember the disguises of your loves.

Swan and Dove

Mate with a god, whatever his disguise,
insistent swan or cool, descending dove.
Why do immortals choose a dress of lies
to cloak desire for girls desiring love?
For each, one meeting in a lifetimes days
made cross-bred scions of earth and paradise,
a doomed inheritance we recognize,
a daughter's beauty, dazzling human eyes,
a burdened son, born to be more than wise.
But Leda? Mary? What charmed memory stays
to last through life's despairs, through mortal's praise,
or what cold hatred for both swan and dove?

The Looking-Glass

I. *Reflections*

How did I see myself,
learn my image,
in the first days of time?

I learned to recognize
my face in another's eyes.

. . .

How did I learn, alone
to change myself
to wear a crown, a garland?

I looked into a pool
I dipped my fingers in the water
meaning to cup my hands to drink.
I saw myself
wreathed by the reflected summer grasses.

. . .

At last they made a mirror out of polished bronze
where I could see my youth,
then silver mirrors for my silks and gold;
and last a looking glass that does not blur the truth
where I, once young, will watch myself grow old.

II. *Daphne*

How should a girl, walking in a forest,
laughing with lighthearted friends,
know the footsteps following her footsteps
were a god's, pursuing?

How should a girl, singing in the sunshine,
hearing a voice echoing her song,
know it was a god's, offering to a mortal
a lover's incantation?

How should a god, seeing a girl in terror,
believe she would choose death rather than love,
see in her eyes no god but fear's cold shadow,
strange to his wooing?

How should a laurel tree, dressed in blossom,
bending its branches to a weeping god,
know that he believes she is a woman
who knows his desolation?

III. *The Flower Wife*

There was a man, a prince, who had no wife.
His friends made charms to build a girl from flowers
they wove her flesh from spring,
her voice from birdsong and her tears from dew.
She stepped, surprised, into warm human life.
But when she knelt to look into a stream
she saw herself, made from spell and dream.
How should she live beyond a summer day?
Live longer than the plants from which she grew
that winter gathers and snow hides away?.

IV. *The Looking-Glass*

This glass on the palace wall
is dark as water
in any stream or pool.
This glass holds images
as eyes hold them.
Mirror, or water, or glance
capture then loose each face,
but keen no trace
of those who looked, as I,
to see myself in this place
where a hundred candles' light
blazed above banquet or dance.
Do ghosts walk here at night,
do strangers who come here by chance
look, as I look, in the glass
and leave, as I leave, no trace
in the dark-as-water glass?

Nothing there

There was a pool so dark I did not know
what its depths held, what secret lay below.
I sank a shaft; it reached to rock and sand –
nothing but stone, the substance of the land;
no wreck, no treasure, no meshed roots or weeds
to weave their shadows to the sedge and reeds.
From unpolluted water, darkly clear
I stooped to draw and drink my cup of fear.

A brink of shadow

Here is a brink of shadow, age or hope,
but which it is I cannot recognize
though I must be my own interpreter
if there is any meaning to be found
or any message to be understood.
Here senses move alert, curious, not at ease
for nothing's blurred, nothing dulled by use,
nothing wears custom as an old disguise,
no other's words clothe this experience.
Here I must be my own interpreter.

At early morning, under a clear sky,
I, as a stranger, walk in a dell of grasses
seeing and touching, newly arrived,
solitary in a strange continent
where all is unaccustomed.
I am a stranger, one who has forgotten
all of life, needing it no more:
seeing it without memory, so without meaning,
looking, turning away
to cross a brink of shadow, hope or time.

This solitude

The solitude I own is hard as rock
made like rock of infinitessimal lives
fragments of plants, voices of distant summers
ashes that warmed a winter room at night.
This fossil trace was a bird's quill, that one a fish
and both knew movement in the elements
and both make part of a stone
which hands may carve or build into a tower.

The solitude I own is also prison;
each hour or season binds me to myself
or to my shadow that walked in freedom once.
How can I remember
which fishes leapt the shining waterfall
in woods that smelt of moss and rainy days?
which birds were singing when I gathered fruit?
which branches built a fire which turned to stone
as I to solitude?

No hand in the night

No hand in the night
gives reassurance if I wake in tears
or breaks the boundary of nightmare fears.
Solitude, with whom I live,
Silence, our other, cold companion,
watch in the house, wait in my room:
when night dissolves their dark disguise
they stay inside the door to guard my day
where their long shadows lie across the years.

Clocks and Times

When the clock stops, time does not cease
though heartbeat ticks no longer stir
an empty and deserted house,
hours continue night and day
and do not stay.

When time ends, when joy breaks down
every boundary and wall,
or death makes silence stretch so long
a stillness round a living grief,
the clock goes on, the circling hands
never pause, do not acknowledge
they measure nothing as they turn.

Dialogue

'For every wound time cannot heal
reveal no sign but bear the mark,
For every night of tears, conceal
the story of the long-drawn dark.'

'For every joy and pleasure found
walk lightly, so your footsteps show
their flowery passage on bare ground,
though why flowers spring no-one must know.'

'Secret in all your thoughts, yet give
with every sense to all who need,
so take from life the strength to live,
to love in every word and deed.'

'All this is known, yet failure walks
complacent, at a shadow's pace,
listening where every gossip talks,
mocking at all desire for grace.'

Stage Settings

Places were where we went; we changed the places,
scenes for our play, light on us, with us fleeting,
but ever afterwards the town had secret faces,
each street that had been setting for our meeting.

I came to you through snow with snow on hair and hand,
then our dark footsteps marked a wide stone stair
unused by any other passers-by,
even wind made way for us, sheathing its knifed air.

Or shade fell on us from a new-fledged tree
shut in the garden of a city square,
blossoming backdrop for our meeting's silence
so unperceived it might not have been there.

Meetings and partings gone, the places stay
for whose encounters? Yours and mine no more;
someone will use them for another play
and speak the same words that we spoke before.

Fast bind, fast find

Each time the scar is shown the wound recedes,
the pain more blunted and the fear grown stale,
neither is conjured by a story's needs,
tissue and skin have closed and clothed to heal.
Colour of time, shock, courage, panic cease
as speech acknowledges a full release.

And pictures blur a face in all its moods,
they cannot smile to meet the living eye
nor change to answer thought or tears or words,
exact or in interpreting they lie.
For sight was matched with moment and each sense
took part to shape the seen's full consequence.

So truth is changed each time the past is told,
diminishing as years draw out in length,
a different shimmer lights the unchanging gold.
So hide the scars if you would keep pain's strength,
and never look at pictures of the dead
and never say again what's once been said.

Take my hand, dancer

Take my hand, dancer,
I take your hand.
See, the different flesh, yours dark, mine pale;
see the shapes, strong thumbs, nimble fingers,
whorls of skin patterns, no two in the world alike,
and the lines of life, the lines of fate,
under the differing flesh the matching structure of bone.

Take my hand, dancer,
like yours it has held bread and fruit,
knife and cup;
like yours it has touched earth and water.
See, there is nothing strange
in my hand, in your hand
that meet to hold us together
while the music guides our footsteps.
Why should either distrust, dance-long, life-long,
the meaning of the other
whose hands are as like the leaves of a single tree?

Trees

Consider trees as creatures of their own
– not fruit or fire or shelter for mankind –
see them in forests, orchards, or alone
with idiom of each species well defined.

All move to music of a range too deep
for us to recognise or comprehend:
their branches dance or meditate or weep
gestures that speak and phrases they intend.

Their saraband starts with light-blowing seed,
a winged life for the ash and sycamore,
plane tree's broken orb, nut's kernel freed
or rotted fruits feeding the pip-brimmed core.

For years, for decades or for centuries
roots go searching to nourish and sustain
a season's need for leaves, and each leaf dies
yet all new summers bring new leaves again.

As roots pierce darkness under grass and ground
branches declare this music, so fulfil
beyond our scope, song that has no sound,
dance most apparent when the dancer's still.

Weep for dead trees

After night-frost spikes of grass are glassy,
an acorn cup carries no fruit inside,
three strands of berries twist black with red, with scarlet,
ivy wreaths bare tree-trunks in the wood,
rime outlines leaves layered on the ground,
downhill, mist smoothes the change from land to water.
Which are the dead, which the living trees?
Only beeches wear last year's sapless leaves
dried to metal colours by the cold.
Masked by winter, dead trees stand with living
ranked together in their tracery:
these dead, sheltered by life's companionship,
will be discovered when the spring buds open
in summer leafage, in manifold green bounty
pierced by branches
savage as the naked bones of death.

The Late Brood

There's a black garland by the blocked-in well,
dead winter leaves I thought, rain-soaked and torn,
but when I looked again it was all birds,
their arrow-pointed wings draggled and worn,
twig legs, stained beaks, but here and there
one pure feather fitted for the air
lay on the stone perfect and forlorn,
a message from decay sharper than words.

Rainbird

Because all birds and birdsongs here are strange
for songs I hear I must invest the birds.
For tunes that draw small circles in the air
tumble, cascade and use a fountain's words,
hidden in branches dangling chains of fruit,
I draw a creature that is small and crested,
hovering and curvetting in the shade,
grey as water, white and silver breasted.

Books would name it and describe the species,
but in this garden with its plumaged grasses,
laced butterflies and lizards dragon-headed
I listen as the rain draws near and passes.
This small spring of song in the trees' shadow
gives Eden back, with all things still unknown;
because I cannot name them, they are nameless
and this wild garden is the world I own.

Fort Aguada Beach

A man, ragged as a beggar, and his bear
left the quilted shade palms spread on sand
as if it were another century
or a memory
from which they came into full, noonday heat.

They treat each other without any trust.
He'd tied the creature to half-close its mouth
it plodded after him, roped to his hand.
Its fur, harsh, black and winter-thick,
its eyes questioning,
its body answering to rope and stick.
Bound to each other's fear
they are each other's livelihood.

Beach idlers under tasselled canopies
laugh to see the creature stand
begging for their laughter.

Being estranged from beggary's endurance
I cannot speak a word either will understand,
knowing no common language but a coin.

Devised by love

Devised by love when language is strange speech
creatures invent caresses for a human,
their claws drawn in or heads bowed to a hand
asking for touch to meet their own devotion.
Even a bird, imprisoned in a cage,
will take a finger boldly in its beak
to gentle it, forgiving captivity.

When wilder creatures, disregarding fear,
accept us, as they do another breed,
sharing the sunlight or the winter stress
we feel as honoured by indifference
as by the invention of their gentleness.
We guess at meanings left as far behind
as the shared ages of evolving life,
discarding words that cloak the human mind
we recognise their gestures by our own.

At Panjim

A mermaid fountain whitely commands the square,
those other squares have saints or conquerors,
halo or helmet to preside and bless.
I ask her story. Everyone forgets
whether she saved a vessel in distress
or brought some glorious harvest to the nets
but one last votary loves her curled, stone hair.

When he was young he fished these moon-shoaled seas.
Along this coast young men are fishermen,
women, dressed in flower and fire colours,
twist their thin dresses high above their knees,
sell the bright catch under the market trees
while the men sleep in the palm shades of home.

Now, in the shadow of the governor's palace,
he crouches on the pavement at his work.
Age has made him a landsman: for his solace
he cuts slim fishes from grey strips of horn,
precisely lines each fin and tail and eye,
then, with a file, makes each a mermaid's comb.

Galatea to Pygmalion

You made a synthesis of form and stone,
you called me woman, made my beauty whole
and capable of grace: a lingering glance
caught in stillness, a climax of a dance;
for each limb's surface postulates the bone.
You set me on a plinth of leaf and scroll
but in my eyes you ventured on a soul.

I grew from outside inwards, as you broke
chippings from marble to reveal your hope;
memory fed your eyes, eyes served your hands.
You spoke to Love, 'See where my creature stands,
let her perfections house your utmost scope.'
Who answered when your cold ambition spoke?
I do not know: I only know I woke.

I could not learn my senses by their growth
for I possess no minute nor no day.
I had no blinding, deafening, bruising hour of birth
no change from helpless limbs groping to earth
for foothold, handhold, perspective for my way.
Though I stand here as flesh and flower of youth
I have no promise, no memory, no truth.

I stand unmoving though no longer stone,
still the deliberate beauty of your dream,
achievement known before the work could start,
heartless before your too demanding heart.
Wish all undone. Wish that I still seem
remote, unbodied or broken and undone.
Wish me still vision and yourself alone.

Once upon a time

In old days, in stories that begin
'Once upon a time', nothing was strange;
Some spoke with wolves or eagles, heard trees talk
leaf against leaf, murmuring news from far
till small birds gossiped it about the sky
and though men might not understand the words
they knew it was a language.
But now our flocks and herds
are things that we have shaped and made,
they have no fighting and no mating season
but wait for us to breathe the breath of life
into their metal frames
not once but hourly, till they break.
If we listen till they rust away
we'll hear no secrets of the world from them.

The garden metaphor

The garden metaphor for Paradise entices
as leaves unfold in everlasting spring
while orchards glow with long, autumnal bounty
in shady coverts for nightingales to sing,
each shady, grassy, flowering, secret place
where lovers walk with friends in casual grace.

The garden metaphor hides facts discovered –
bird's living food, flytrap, web, sundew,
while golden creatures feed on carrion prey
or crouch to spring in copse or avenue.
Accept dead flesh and steely, watching eyes
before you name the garden Paradise.

Human

When I lived in a different time,
in a rotting house,
in poverty, ignorance and by the seasons
I did not know my ignorance,
I did not recognize misery,
it was as it was.
Then I learned new words: I saw as a shadow,
as a sickness, myself and my house.
I saw my poverty, my lack of knowledge;
being so informed I chose,
I found my way to another place.
Nothing else would have been possible
after I understood my need.
But I look back to my dark ignorance,
past generations of my changing state
and remember other things,
wondering if cockcrow and harvest
are not the images of content.

Limitations

Prologue

There's no one here:
houses behind the hill
lie in the sun and sleep.
This stony autumn cannot pasture sheep,
the flowers are seedheads for the winds to reap,
brown grass roots linger for the winter rain.
No birds are near;
waves speak, all else is still
where staring sea and sky
face each other in perpetual gaze.
So I thought, listening,
so I thought, idling in solitude and light.

But then I saw
that every curve and flaw
in rock or bent or tree
was living infinitely,
growing and dying was what I looked upon.
For beetle's track, a floating thistledown,
a ripening berry or a broken shell
were a great language, words I could not spell
nor guess at what they tell
in speech and idiom unknown to me.

Seasons and stars or shadows of a plant,
sands long smoothing in the sea's salt palm,
what calculation do these mark or own?
And what recording grains or shapes a stone
that's chosen path for hurrying, burdened ant,
or where a sunning fly in lazy calm
spreads wings that match the lichens, grown
in cutting tracery and close as flesh to bone?

And deeper still, can moss seem like a tree
to something smaller than my eyes can see
some creature lesser than my touch can find,
below the scale of sight or scope of mind?

Small

In the distortion of a summer thought
slug, aphid, ant, and all the garden creatures
grew to monsters-till each joint, eye, scale
was magnified into-a dragon's features.
I, their destroyer, a patron of the roses,
diminished to an insect's minute being
saw them, great pasturing herds, all afternoon:
and ever since, instructed by this seeing,
I questioned the condition of my power.
Their dying is a pain too small to see,
their cries are pitched too high for human ears.
I bring them death so flowers shall pleasure me
and feel no claim of brotherhood for tears.

Hidden

Tulip, lily and wild rose
flower in valleys seldom seen
where the mountains and the cold
in chains of ice and rock withhold
these fragile creatures flowering.
Travellers have found this green
tapestried with sudden spring
unseen, unused: yet there unfold
tulip, lily and wild rose.

Each stem leaping from the ground
sectioned, magnified and drawn
shows precision and design
architectural in line,
gothic vaulting, tracery.

So each grass-blade in a lawn
hides structural mastery,
in each leaf-vein patterns found,
each stem leaping from the ground.

Large

A telescope sweeps through the night,
lens where my eyes grow great in sight;
miles vanish into measureless,
space makes speed seem motionless,
night's mysterious dimension
makes star and planet dark's invention
for where are they in daylight if unseen?
Where is Arcturus when the grass is green?

Unknown

From small, unseen and huge I must infer
we are enclosed by sense's limitation,
myopic eyes and the astronomer
being the limits of one variation –
dumb to singer, or, if you consider
hearing better choice for indication,
one can hear bat's cry, thinner than a whisper,
yet be deaf to crying of a nation.

So what are we who cannot measure pain?
and who are we before we come to birth?
We do not know the language of the earth
or guess how trees feel in the winter rain,
our limits fixed by heartbeat and by breath,
our boundaries are known as love and death.

Lyke Wake Dirge

Understanding death comes too late for speech,
a backward look can be the utmost given
life's values slip so simply out of reach.

So we, the watchers soon to be mourners, riven
by grief, relief, or cold from lack of sleep,
worn by endurance almost hear, see even,

presences in the room our senses keep:
outside our boundaries become aware
– even while our bodies shudder, crouch and weep –

of other traffic in a different air.
Experiencing any hour of death
we learn the rumours of another-where,

and apprehend beyond a failing breath
images of romance: the stony road,
the barren thorn trees of an endless heath,

question and answer; all the heavy load
of a life's days now to be summed and weighed
past chasms bridged by threads not footstep broad.

Bring water, flowers, and then cold linen, laid
in quiet folds upon the useless thing
while some formality of prayers are said,

though all the while our thoughts as journeying,
accompanying the stranger who has gone
and moves unseen on foot or air or wing.

We must suppose that shackles are undone,
accept escape from all time's use and wear,
jealous of knowledge, still, to us, unknown
and angry in the sorrow we must bear.

Memorial Service

His ageing widow dreams of youth,
his sons stand in their father's place,
his friends translate him to a stone,
sisters recall his childhood face,
so quickly death confuses truth.
He lies in state, corrupt, alone.

Though hopes and fears are multiplied
boredom blunts pain and stifles doubt,
words weave a dream of light and life.
His widow rises like a bride
comes down the aisle, leads the dark rout
and greets her friends as death's new wife.

The First Martyr

I

Someone must go first across the sea,
or make new words, language of voice and heart,
must build, name stars, first think eternity.

So in each life there's always some new start,
learning to touch and taste, to speak and hear,
first time to meet and then first time to part.

Later there's recognition, fear names fear,
love finds that love can be no other light,
truth once known makes its abundance clear.

When Stephen faced the stoning winter night,
his miracles, his healing, love all spent
he was the first to claim a martyr's right

to blaze the path by which all others went.

II

'Death, the presence that we do not own,
is now beside me,
a cloak of tattered pain to hide me,
torn flesh and broken bone.
My fear – almost fear I do not fear,
my shadow hand wards off a shadow stone.
The last experience, the last of need,
a shred of time, before being wholly freed
to know the light, the love is truly known
to bless deliverance, to bless the falling stone.'

III

One must go first for others to be sure
there is a road, so conquering their fear
they use his strength for patience to endure:

and more than this, the martyrdoms appear
as miracles, defeating torture, fires,
bearing more pain than human frame can bear

because the light to which their love aspires
comes sooner than the lived-out span of years
to free them from a bondage that devours.

They give forgiveness and they need no tears.

Archaeology

From pure lines of the skeleton
we cannot tell what flesh once grew,
delicate or coarse, upon the bones,
nor find a clue to its-humanity;
saint and traitor must look alike at last
and love leaves no more trace than poverty.
But from a buried city's artefacts
we resurrect a race.

The Inheritor

Prologue

High sun, full noonday, where my shadow's cast,
this is my day, my strength: the years I climb
reach to achievement, if I turn back, look down.
I know myself heir to each ruined town,
harbourmaster to the wrecks of time,
rememberancer to my world for all the past.

I walk among the ruins, gaze at broken stone,
touch coin and cup, read man's silenced speech,
names of conquests, name of king and state,
trace roads through deserts to a city gate,
to the last dispossession I may reach,
the intimate sadness of some light, fragile bone.

The City

I know myself heir to each ruined town . . .

No map names this place nor marks its being.
These mounds and hollows might be nothing more
than natural rock under the wavering grass,
ripples of flowers then their falling seed.
Wild bees make honey in a hollow tree,
snakes find small, sun-warmed ledges where they coil;
ants build their citadels and corridors . . .
this little world of late-come citizens
inherits here, inhabits here, survives
the long obliterate traces of mankind.

The long obliterate traces of mankind
return from darkness as we excavate,
give back to daylight street and market place.
We find the temples and the names of gods,
shrines where blessing follows sacrifice,
little votive offerings of hope
scattered, scattered, all their wishes lost,
lost as their voices singing or whispering.

The Wine Shop

Where did the orchards and the vineyards grow?

A laughing mask
above a doorway,
broken cups strew a burned clay floor,
wine jar, wine cask . . .
All these recall
a village tavern
where plane trees shade
is lightly spread
over bench and table:
a place to idle,
to drink, to talk,
for village gossip,
for evening songs . . .
remembered scent
of baking bread,
a table spread
with a woven cloth,
a plate of olives
a glass of wine.
I look again
at the broken jar,
at the laughing mask . . .
I know, I share
all that was here.

Where did the orchards and the vineyards grow?

Lost at Sea

Bright flocks of fishes move in weightless ease
where broken ships spill cargoes on the sand,
discharge their bullion, lost to history.
Who may inherit this strewn legacy,
take a Phoenician coin in his hand,
take up a broken sword where all wars cease?

Sea flowers, sea monsters guard the depths and caves;
like empty shells man's small remains lie here
rocked by the water's deeply stirring tide.
Our searching hands probe, extricate, divide,
uncover lightly what was lost in fear
then sank to rest below the restless waves.

The Mound Burial

Dear love at rest
I lay a flower by your hand,
a head of yarrow,
all I could find
in this cool land
as summer ends.
Dear love, you lie
slender as shadow
that sleeps on grass
below a winter tree.
When night's dark falls
the shadow goes
as you have gone.
Now earth must be
your coverlet.
My flower lies
beside your hand.
Remember summer,
dear love, in death,
as I, lifelong,
must remember today
when summer ended.

Avenues and Circles

Storytellers say these stones were dancers
because they pair in avenue and circle:
what was the music to which they might have danced?

Storytellers say these stones were dancers.
Masked in granite, no faces turn in greeting,
cloaked in limestone, no hands meet to touch,
if there was laughter it is hushed and hidden,
creeping grasses bind their feet to stillness
because there is no music for their dance.

Where did the rumour start – that these were dancers?
What midnight caught them in its power for harm?
Who saw the figure end, heard music close?
Who mourned their absence, searched the dancing places
but found no son or daughter, dark or fair,
only stone pillars in avenue or circle,
tall as soldiers, creatures without faces?

Storytellers say these stones were dancers;
dare they believe that stones once moved to music
that lured, or drove or charmed
these mountain splinters here to watch the moon,
to foretell all her phases, her eclipse?

The Museum

In these tall rooms
we walk through history.

Spears and shields once marked and stained with blood
are ranked in order, outlasting their old wars,
tortures and betrayals eased to silence;
while those who fought for long-changed boundaries
are lost beyond all courage, fear and pain.

Beauty's jewels will not be worn again,
nor household goods be used at any hearth.
Clay cups will not hold water, gold cups wine,
hunger and thirst and feasting are all ended
for those whose strewn possessions have been found
under the waves, under the haunted ground.

In these tall rooms
gods are assembled,
creators and destroyers without power.
They gaze at crowds who are not worshippers,
who know their fables, who do not come for blessing.

Patterns of life, no stranger than our own,
assembled here piece out a map of time,
landscapes inhabited by many dead
whose faces and whose voices are unknown.

In these tall rooms I find the world I have inherited.

Search

What's left, what's kept, what's undisturbed by time?
The leaves fall down, deepening last year's leaves;
thoughts wear no mark of use, no chisel's trace;
echo cannot break silence with new speech
nor a demolished house reclaim its place
nor man remake the web a spider weaves.

Take a small vertebra or rib – can bone
tell what the creature was in hide or pelt,
name cries no longer carried on the wind?
Echo lies still and dead flesh knows no pain.
Hope finds no foothold in a language spelt
by signs that offer nothing to the mind.

The change was gradual: stone by painful stone,
carried by iron when the beasts were dead,
hands hoisted upward to a bridging arch.
But stones fall down upon all history's stones.
Words shout through space, but who hears what is said?
The moon's a garden when the deserts parch.

What's left of falling leaves and falling stone?
Memory builds both tree and tower too high,
recalls a panther wreathed in dancing vines,
renames all knowledge and revives all hope.
Thought was scrawled and then obliterate signs,
its shadow writes no message to the sky.

Before whose time?

Before whose time am I alive
so shall not read their words or hear their music?

How can I lean over the great curve of years
to speak my gratitude to those who lived before me,
to say 'I hear, I hear,'
to those who taught me life?

To have lived before the lightening words
were written on the surfaces of time,
to have died before I saw the pictures
that led my sight and taught me comprehension
would not have seemed a life of famine:
but having known plenty I must wonder
how they endured and perished
before the incantations.
Some will wonder about us
seeing deeper into life than we have done
because of words, of pictures, of sounds we have not known.

History

Wise to define the sources and the safeguards,
building walls and authorising gates,
laying down roads – acknowledgement of journeys –
appointing guardians of whom we ask protection.

Too much for us to take all varied regions
into our keeping: rulers must be established,
served or disobeyed, honoured or disregarded;
unless we have them there's no choice of conduct.

So there are muses for each discipline,
there are gods commanding sacrifice,
there are virtues with their shadow sins,
all points of reference on our map of time
although the boundaries of honour change.

Earth turns and dances on a path in space
while we are certain that we stand upright.

The Prisoner

The prisoner's hand knew every stone,
the broken curve of fossil shell,
low arch and crooked flags that tell
shape and dimension of his cell
where he was captive and alone.

And soon his sight had learned to stay
brooding on lintel, bar or boss
on each green hair of dripping moss,
each shadow-change that crept across
the grille of light that was his day.

The prisoner's ear learned subtle sound,
the crack of ice, far fall of rain,
grief and fear that weep in vain,
strange voices crying through his brain
like creeping rumours of the ground

His mouth found bread's dark taste of rye,
his lips the thirst foul waters hold.
His body ached with ceaseless cold,
corruption of dank stone and mould,
tossed in the fevers of his stye.

No freedom sets the prisoner free;
although the chains fall at his feet
and doors give back the day, the street
where voices speak and strangers meet.
Are they the shadows or is he?

He left no sign, but chains must bind
a weight of sorrow in his place.
His footsteps echo, pace by pace.
And where is he that left no trace?
Captive in dungeons of his mind.

Underground

'Once,' she said, looking at cave-concrete walls,
the hidden light that's opaque, unchanging,
'once there were birds . . .
there were seasons then, of long days and of short,
there were soft-falling rains and driving sleet,
delicate, flying snow that could turn brutal . . .'
'But the birds?' they said. She said, 'They flew,
and every species had a different flight;
some were small and brilliant in the sun,
some huge and some lived on the water.
Each species had a language or a song,
perhaps an oboe sound or clarinet
might reach the sound of that most secret language.
Old languages, written on stone or clay
could be unravelled as our scholars found,
telling how many slaves there were
what wine or oil stored within the jars
before the siege or fire in which the cities fell.
'Birdsong,' she said, 'was scrolled upon the air,
and birds,' she said, 'sang mostly in the spring
when days grew longer and leaves and flowers came,
when there was growth and change,
not the unliving and unchanging flowers you know
that cannot bud or die.'
'The birds?' they said, persistent.
'Clothed in feathers peculiar to each race,
their legs as thin as twigs, hard beaks for prey,
bright eyes . . . they lived mysterious and proud,
they crossed the seas and continents in flocks
returning year by year to sing and sing.
Some hunted in the night on gliding wings,
some of the seabirds cried like the wind at night.
In the early day,' she said, 'that was called morning
they crowded with the light into a web of singing:

waking, listening, I could half remember
the meaning of each thread of song.
It meant a memory of all springs before,
or a far country they and I had known:
I can remember it, remembering the time
when there were birds.'

Dona Nobis Pacem

You see an army going to a war
their cause acclaimed but never understood.

Hope shines as bright as banners in the morning
on lance or rifle: it is all the same,
stone, steel or fire have served destruction's scope.

Brother unknown
your hope was mirror image of my own.

By nightfall some must be maimed flesh,
health turned to pain
fear become familiar as thirst,
the cause an echo, almost lost
beyond a desert of uncounted hours.

Brother unknown
your wounds are mirror image of my own.

Beside the frontier where the murders start,
let us disarm each other, for our cause
is known, is understood
because our hope is measured by our loss.

Let us redress the wrong before it's done;
speak to me here and listen to my words,
let us absolve each other of the past.

Brother unknown
your truth is mirror image of my own.

Peace after War . . .

Here is a desert, not a promised land,
where many widows have all time to mourn,
wounds measure out its territory of pain
while derelict weapons rust away the waste
of riches that bought grief instead of grain.
Winner and loser, though each hope was born
of pride and courage, stand humanly disgraced;
victory's a bloodstain on an empty hand.

Cenotaph

Old men march to well-remembered music,
their bodies strive to match each martial tune,
old wounds ache, marking another winter.
Young soldiers think of fear, encompassed and survived.
Young women's tears fall in new solitude,
they cannot guess their loneliness is shared,
or know old women weep for loves as young as theirs,
for separate names of battles spin one shroud for grief.

Has it not all been said?

Has it not all been said and all been told,
charted and measured, criticised, re-made,
so that the chafing, scars, the strands of rope
woven, re-woven by the writer's trade
until all's threadbare, show there's no more scope
only old recognitions to unfold?

Can more be said about the state of joy?
it's known to sing in each distended vein
when hearts for long untouched, for long mere means,
lift, as if winged and liberated, sign
their scrawl of gold across the usual scenes
in lightning that discovers to destroy.

Every human says these same words over;
each city's built upon a city's fall,
all like in purpose. Each succeeding age
varies the script, yet each could speak for all
writing the names they know on history's page,
changeless names of enemy or lover.

Welcoming enemies

There's a new inclination, it is half shame,
half furtive hope, welcoming enemies
and asking for their bounty.
Earthquake, avalanche and storm and flood,
cold, with crazed fingers set in frost, to trap
tramp, climber, bird, straying indoor creatures;
all disasters known since words were made
therefore familiar; but unpredictable, therefore strange,
return and claim your victims.
You prototypes of named and unnamed gods of darkness
stretching your claws from every underworld
or bending from the whirlwind's canopy
without apparent justice, mercy, choice,
take your tythe: we offer you ourselves.
We have made arms of power and pain,
tortures and tyranny, weapons of fire;
the skill that serves us makes the death we serve
and traps us in our own intelligence.
So we must ask for all we cannot tame
the old, impartial enemies, to hurt us, hunt us
and force us back into each other's love.

What was the kingdom?

What was the kingdom?
An acre, or an island, or an age.

What was the crown?
Impossible justice married to tyranny.

What was the power?
Of life and death, no more.

What were the city walls?
All dead men's bones.

What was the river's flood?
Some said tears, some rain; but it was blood.

What was the happiness?
A single tree.

What was the city's name?
I cannot tell
for it had many names before it fell.

The Crystal Skull

All pain converges in the hidden brain,
instant communication from the eye
spreads a net to catch these mortal tears.
        Why are the innocent birds shut in small cages.

Wounds inflicted on the heart or flesh,
torture, devised to break truth or silence,
are not exalted by exalting pain,
        although stone martyrs decorate the door.

If pain's endurance is recognized redemption
it is exalted to a means of grace,
disguised as love to trespass in that kingdom
        to mock the rose by a dead wreath of thorn.

I see the reason for this crystal skull,
this shape that copies bone, but bone conceals
the brain that grew to meditate on pain,
        This crystal holds the light and nothing more.

Nocturne

The lulling absolution of the sea
accepts the swimmer into summer peace
lapping each sense in moon's refracted light,
or, in the phosphorescence of the night,
disguised in fire within the night's release
to float where stars define immensity.

This is the peace of unpossessing hands,
quiet illusion of a solitude:
for underwater, where sea-grasses move
and corals arch in formal glade and grove,
life has its kingdoms and its multitude
and other languages and other lands.

No footsteps mar the water, mark this place,
yet solitude is limited by sight
and silence by the scope of human ear.
What music moves beyond the sounds I hear,
what suns careen beyond the edge of night,
what bastions isolate the mortal race?

Rock me, dark seas of wisdom and of night;
rumours of music rise beyond your waves,
rise from your silence interlaced with stars,
recall dominion that day's knowledge bars,
an incantation that absolves and saves
flooding the dark and burning into light.

Last Poems

Autumnal

Winter will dress me soon in snow, in fear, in stillness.
I turn from that cold glass to find another crystal
retrace the way I chose to time I choose.
It lies in secret. hidden under days;
long drifts of coloured leaves or coloured hours
blow down the paths, blow down the corridors,
footsteps are heartbeat echoes of my thoughts,
my thoughts remake an image of the house.

Who sleeps there now?
who sits waiting, waiting?
For what stranger does the light break in
announcing morning?
I have slept here and woken to new days
I have danced here, I can see
tall shadows moving in a patterned maze,
a waft of silk, a shimmering of dawn,
a long soliloquy of happiness.

Mirage, mirage . . . was this once my truth?
Vanish, vanish . . . do not form again,
outline no hope, define no tear, recall no touch,
I am beyond your reach,
no longer waiting, no longer with the dancers.

My hands were pale and smooth,
now bent and brown, now many-ringed with gold,
they loose their skills, release my hoarded joy.

Broken windows of a roofless house
let in moonlight, moonlight unmasks the shadows
where drifting snow lies heaped in silence, silence.

Odyssey

He, returned from war
from years of voyaging
and tired endurance
remembered, as he spoke of seafaring,
faces, voices, sorceries.
Neither guessed those fireside words
echo through centuries
naming all dangerous quests.

The Echo

When you were young
you would not love me.
I was your danger,
hawk to your songbird,
hound to your hare,
heron when you swam, silver as water,
changing disguises you could not lose me.

Now, when you choose me,
claiming allegiance
wrapped in your age,
flesh fails beauty,
disguise completed
pursuit defeated,
I cannot answer,
nor will I speak of love to a stranger.

Street Scene

Boys and girls have cut and dyed their hair
some half-shaved heads are crested brilliant green,
fans of scarlet, sunflower-yellow spikes
with little, silver dangles in between.
aureoletheir delicate, their painted features
where eyes look out from diamonds drawn in black
Violet lips are heart shaped, or new moons.
They wear their pretty faces above rags
but clothe their legs in colours like their hair,
jewel their fingers to glitter in the sunlight.
They're humming birds and birds of paradise
flocking the streets, flights of fantastic creatures,
woodpecker laughter, shouts like crow or jay.
These are the birds that cannot fly away.

Two Saints

Beautiful girls, Chiara, loving Francis
barefoot for his sake, transmuting, if she did,
love of him to love of charity,
lies dead, old aged, for seven centuries:
while Zita, who was she? fades on an altar,
veiled and garlanded with paper roses,
silks rotting like Chiara's austere robe.
Beauties, beauties, death's decencies denied,
stay exposed to every curious eye
as blackened flesh of poor mortality.

The Moral of the Story

The cold princess, wasting on an ice-mountain
hoped a brave lover would achieve the climb,
one who would win her, save, unfreeze, limb by limb
her winter years and make her young again.
None were so strong. Her vigil was in vain.

So, if you want as much, are not content with less
than the first morning dream, than aspiration
to find a life that will engross and bless
and watch all hope wither to desperation
do not suppose intention for the best
was less than wise. Stay on your mountain crest.

Dreams

The Rose Hedge.

I saw the growing hedge
a myth of rose and thorn,
one side shone with sunlit day
where we had been for ever.
When the leaves parted
for my unwilling way
you stayed shadowless, alone,
as I returned to night
holding this shred of memory
like grassblade or a flower.

The Weeping Man.

The weeping man I could not comfort
might not tell his grief.
Because I held him in my arms
my sorrow found relief.

Landscape.

Bastions of rock were certainly a city
unlit and distant on the cliffs of night,
clouds, defined by movement, blowing
above a plain of lesser stones and boulders
where fear should have inhabited with space and silence.
I was alone, clothed in exaltation
as if all wishes and all hopes were found
as if, in that wide darkness, I was light.

Platonic Myth

As I must go there I invent the scene.
Two springs are named. There is one cypress tree
white as moonlight. I suppose that night
has stolen colour from our darkest green
and all the flowers I might expect to see
crowding the bank must also all be white.

Frost flowers perhaps? They grew on window panes
wreathing morning in lace and fronds of ice,
rootless, scentless, winters garlanding.
Drink here? Then lose all memory that remains,
a new beginning at a heavy price,
a slate washed clean, a famine harvesting.

A meadow is named too. The other spring
is for the brave who'd take all they have found
as burden or as hope where they must go.
Is there perhaps a summer murmuring,
where mortal flowers grow on immortal ground?
This is not told, and there's no way to know.

Will thirst decide where I should dip my hand?
Will some destroying pain before I died
blur loves remembered, joy I had to leave?
I cannot know before if I command
enough of courage and enough of pride
to turn from Lethe's peace and long reprieve.

The Plane Tree in Winter

Familiar tree, a day and night companion,
sight knows so well it moves as hands might move
touching flaked bark in every sort of weather.
Leaning branches and their pendant twigs
break from the trunk, stemming from earth to air.
Stripped by autumn from a weight of leaves
it shows no common bond with vertebrates,
but, winter-bared, knows naked liberation
for light or rain or snow to decorate
beyond comparison with jewels, gold or tears .
Night draws it black against a lamplit sky,
a garden guardian, guardian of my sleep.
Summer lodged lightly in its pride of leaves;
easy as birds, in any season,
thoughts, quick as wings, have rested in its shelter.

Required reading

Princesses in those stories had no names
the title gave them beauty, jewelled cloaks,
sometimes captivity, sometimes advantages,
gifts given at birth, doweries of hope.
It all seemed simple and likely to be fact,
to ride white horses with a chosen hero
under the branches of great orchard trees,
the apples being gold, but to be eaten,
or listen to the messages birds brought,
to keep the little walnut with great care
knowing it held balldress and dancing slippers
so you, adventuring in dishonoured rags,
could dance, be recognized, set the false rival weeping
because at last the prince saw you as truth,
claimed you and gave you half his shining kingdom,
fountains and peacocks and eternal youth.

These threads have made both tapestries and cobwebs,
a moonlit park with skeletons of trees
where ghosts still walk, sighing for lost lovers.
The birds on shadow wings have crossed the seas.

Changes

I

The Cave

Stumbling by torchlight through a re-found cave
I find ancestral drawings on the rock
of fellow-owners of old plains and pastures.
Red, above broken antlers and their murdered bones,
they race or crouch or feed: familiar features
of enemies or of a pastoral flock,
recorded memories, companion creatures
known to the hunter's and the herdsman's eye
accurately traced in a dark secrecy.

When? by what torchlight? only one signature,
a single handprint marks an artist's dye,
his outlined hand – usual as yours or mine
though fortune-telling lines are blurred away –
is clear to see. The first human sign
affirming power, or, perhaps a clue
left by a father of the human line
offering all our measured time has known,
his open hand drawn ochre on the stone.

II

Dinosaurs

Roots of memory are deeply set.
It is believed that, long before ma's time,
before he shaped a word or chose a name,
under ice ages, under fossil forests
dragons were buried with those ferns, those thickets
where they had pastured, mated, died,
extinct before our ancestors were born.
Remembrance holds them in a deeper knowledge
than in the burials of pre-history.

Painters remembered dragons, shaped them like dinosaurs,
stories recalled them as enemies and monsters,
dreams made them symbols for interpretation,
like and unlike those innocent beginners
feeding on grasses in an uncharted world.

These creatures of the past are summoned back,
an impress of a foot, dug from a mine,
skulls, vertebrae, even whole skeletons
are reassembled by anatomists,
confronting memories, confronting dreams,
discovering our belief in disbeliefs.

We do not know the colours that they wore,
do not recall their voices, cries or songs
more than we guess the sound of faltering words
when hunters told their children in a firelit cave
"My father's father said that there were dragons."

III

Changes

Our needed gods were summoned, from the sky,
out of the forest or the thundercloud,
to answer supplication, cure calamity.
We made them wayward, powerful and proud
forcing obedience, service, sacrifice.
We knew protection must exact a price.

The story changed, the gods made us from clay
and set us in the garden they'd devised,
left us to learn our lines and act the play;
the scenes were long and mostly ill-advised.
But we stole fire from heaven, fruit from a tree
and turned our thoughts to immortality.

IV

No boundaries

Our boundaries were our senses' limitation,
nothing unheard, unseen, untouched could be,
only our coloured dreams of hope
rose from each deathbed as a contradiction,
taking earth's pattern of returning spring
as an assurance.
Then lenses drew down stars into close vision,
distance, once journey's measure, now seems endless,
infinity stands for eternity.
Microscopes show, delicate, precise,
amazing patterns in all forms of life,
inheritance observed-and catalogued.
No star-robed gods rule a gold paradise.
No underworld waits with its ferryman
and no redemption saves us from ourselves.
We stand as fearful in immensity
as those old ancestors at the cave's mouth,
like them desiring safety and protection.
Our offerings are love we have created,
compassion we have learned, wisdom, of which we know;
We have no shrine where we may lay such tributes.

The Voyager

I was a citizen of earth,
my time and space were easy to define,
clocks measured hours, distances were miles,
sun ruled my daylight, the moon led the tides,
She was the poets' province through all history,
lovers claimed her blessing on their secrecy.

I was her lover in another sense,
lenses showed her man-named continents.
I saw her mountains, craters and her plains.
I dreamed her landscapes, making them my own.

To gain her, claim her for my territory,
I gave my flesh to a hard discipline,
I gave my mind to science, hands to skill,
and won my way to make her conquest mine.

Flight

We were bound
as if for sacrifice.
My breath was fear,
heart beat, battering sound,
hands, cold as ice.
And still.
Last seconds spill
an earth-time past away
till heraldry of flame
burns from the ground.
This was our choice and will.

Journey

From this small cabin, my body's limitation,
I see what none have seen before today,
proving the truth of man's imagination;

cities walled by time, folded away
nature lost beyond interpretation
while colours of the many oceans stay.

Blue world, a landsman gazing from the skies
stares at the clouded globe from which he came
its mysteries closed by distance from his eyes.

There's nothing visible that I can name
though memory searches through the clouds' disguise
and love cries out for all to be the same -
the furthest landfall of known centuries.

Moonwalk

Can man touch barren soil
without supposing trees,
tread among stones and not imagine harvest,
not look for water to sustain all life?

These languages of earth have no place here.

I saw my footprint on the heavy dust,
I saw my shadow darken on the rock,
I saw horizons I had no means to reach,
I saw both hills and plains, bare to the sky.

I heard no echo sigh from any past
for death has never reached or ruled this sphere.

We came as robbers for this dust of time
to gather what lay scattered at our feet,
for purposes remote as speculation
about this desolation
that lies, unrained on, harvestless and cold.

Strange as the world before it stirred with life.

A hope for fear

When I return, a changeling from the sky,
burdened by homesick love, what can I bring
more than these moon rocks from our distant quest?

This cannot be a place for man to live,
the heartbreak memory of green and sea
would haunt to death those immigrants who came
avid for safety from the world they lost.

I, standing here, who wished the moon a kingdom
pursued imagination's magic strangeness,
the mirage sequences of any dream
learn my allegiance to our fading past.
What can this knowledge give to save, in time,
pelt, plumage, fin, birdsong and shadowing leaves,
from my own species' ignorant disregard?

Terror, my teacher, what I have learned I give.
Terror, command us all, teach us to live.

Excuse

Creatures had their world of sky and forest,
water kingdoms, dark to other eyes,
their disciplines of custom and of kind
learned through millenia longer than our time
as were their languages of cry and song.
We, who fight and feud with our own kind,
tamed, killed and used them, for clothing, food or work
used knife, trap, shot, to further our own needs.

No penitence was laid on us for wrong.

What bodies have been used to learn new skills
in transplant, surgery and human ills?
What creatures maimed, testing drugs and germs?
What others caged where wings cannot be spread?
What victims herded, thirsty, starved, to die
in slaughter houses where no death is kind?
In seas, polluted by our human waste
our carelessness prevails beyond our rights.

No penitence is laid on us for wrongs.

God's our excuse who made them, most, to feed
on other living creatures for their lives.
This is his blessing on our traps and knives,
our cruelties and all our heartless greed.

As we forget

We spawn like lemmings we despise
and waste the earth, outlaw each creature,
careless as we kill each other
man is supposed to be man's brother.
Does justice guide our hands and eyes
as we forget and murder nature ?

Civil War

Look at your maps, a table spread
with records, boundaries changed every day
where once-good neighbours fight for once-shared land
blurred by ruins, hedged with unburied dead.
Do you, now enemies, both understand
how many deaths are a fair price to pay
for any acre? Count the yards per head
as once you counted crops of corn or hay
that fed your cattle and made your daily bread.

Biographies

How can we claim to love the dead
changeless, defenceless as they are
when such betraying words are said
whose echoes travel far?
What seemed truth and daily bread
now shows as livid scar.

How can we claim to know the dead
their secrets lost with all they knew –
a fallen tree with leaves long shed –
trifles or treasures, false or true,
a memory's grave, a sleepless bed,
debts long discharged or gifts still due ?

Gone like their voices, not a trace
of touch, of laughter, of repose.
No shadow fills their living space,
what is still hidden? no one knows.
The fragments and a portrait's face
turn to infinities of prose.

Biography as tomb painting

Pacing of hour to hour, of day to day
decades are here all crammed into a book,
pages of pictures decorate the story
show change of child to adult. While you look
young lovers smile, then wither to black silk.
While old companions have their final say.
One more dead friend is filed and put away.

An Alzheimer Case

(for Tony and Ruth)

She is not she: she is as old as I,
bed-ridden mostly, sometimes dressed by others.
She remembers nothing, finds some words
and knows delight, old places all made new,
she is surprised by any flying birds,
by any cloud in any day-time sky.
She is a stranger, I to her, a stranger,
courteous and charming when I take her hand,
but not remembering any love once known
or that, once, she was my new-found-land.

So, is this love? or is this age's cheat,
or time and sickness playing a strange game,
disguise or mask, or gift won from defeat?
Changelings were young in every fairy tale.
She is as old as I and in her sight
I am a visitor she likes to meet,
telling him happy nothings, smiling, glad
of any talk she hears, not understands,
of all she sees: my half-remembered name
she speaks as question when she takes my hands.

Letter from a Stranger

If I'd stooped to the tidemark on the sand,
by winter sea, and wrack-stained, dull, there lay
a small glass bottle waiting to be found
I'd guess it held light words scribbled some summer day
– not now a cry from some wrecked castaway –
then saw my name, a crumpled paper fold
a message from the distance of the dead,
What should I do? What say?
This is the story that a stranger told,
words streamed unguided from his pen, for me,
a letter, intimate, informed and strange
with promises of long held hope and love.
I, who dared not look beyond death's change,
stare wondering at this paper in my hand
asking in doubt and hope if it can prove
time is the tide-washed shore beside my winter sea?

Sanction for love

Sanction for love was given by gods and poets
who taught the words, the necessary truth,
nourished expectation through separate days of youth
leading our journeys to the destined tryst.
We had both served these gods with some attention
in long apprenticeship to work, to love,
but not supposed, in any reasoned thought,
more than we had found upon our ways
making content the substance of our days.
Bewildered by the fortune, pain and joy
meeting bestowed, dazed by recognition,
after what centuries of separation,
dare doubt again, through any grief,
that hope outlasts all questioning disbelief ?

O Western Wind . . .

An anniversary

This was our world's end day, dear love,
an end of time but not of tears,
the end of touch, the silenced word,
the first day of our separate years.
When will time end for me, dear love,
or end for both in darkest night,
or shall I find, in that unknown
your hand is mine, and mine your own?

Remembering Paradise

I can remember paradise,
exiles cannot speak of all that's lost
which silence buries, like the smothering dust
drifted on cities with unrecorded names.

For me it was a place of many flowers,
some I have recognized surviving here,
where friends, word-charmed, delight each other
with wit, with kindness and with dancing grace.
There, and then, creatures knew no fear
nor we of them, bound in a casual liking,
we played together by a gentle sea
each safe, without dependance or captivity.
Magic provision, easy for each want
gave food and drink and sheltering place for rest.
Naked or clothed, the only wearing needed
was tissued light or shadow, as we chose.
For lovers solitudes touch was the wholest sense
that blazed, enclosed, cherished and renewed.

This is the paradise that I remember
finding its traces here, as I might find
one golden earring, lost centuries ago,
gleaming from darkness, still delicate and fine
and, without doubt, make claim that it was mine.

Time being

Time is, time was, time will be, as we play
with variants, mark time, keep time, waste time,
loose time in pastime, hightime, night time, time of day:
these measures flicker through our common speech
as if the word they name, itself, could teach
our haunted actions that there's no escape
from the short lifetime time has power to shape.

Index of Titles

Index of Titles

Index of First Lines

Index of First Lines